Liturgical Music

for the

Revised Common Lectionary

Year **A**

Carl P. Daw, Jr.   •   Thomas Pavlechko

CHURCH PUBLISHING
an imprint of
Church Publishing Incorporated, New York

Church Publishing, Incorporated.
445 Fifth Avenue
New York, New York 10016

www.churchpublishing.com

5 4 3 2 1

THE REVISED COMMON LECTIONARY

This lectionary (RCL) will replace the lectionary in The Book of Common Prayer beginning Advent 2007 and is required for use in the Episcopal church by Advent 2010. The lectionary impacts the schedule of readings appointed for the eucharist and for certain Holy Days: All Saints, Thanksgiving Day, The Presentation, The Annunciation, The Visitation, The Transfiguration, and Holy Cross Day. All other Holy Days in the Episcopal calendar, as well as readings for the daily offices are unaffected.

A feature of the RCL is the two track option for the appointed first readings during the long season of Pentecost beginning with Proper 4. The semi-continuous track offers an in-course reading of selected Old Testament texts and the gospel-related track offers Old Testament texts that are closely related to the appointed gospel. In this *Liturgical Guide* the readings and their subsequent anthems and hymns for the semi-continuous track use are marked "SC Track" and those for the gospel-related track are marked "GR Track". A parish chooses to use one track or the other for the entire season.

AN INTRODUCTION TO THE HYMNS

The hymns listed in this liturgical guide are intended to be a starting place for those who plan Eucharistic worship following the Revised Common Lectionary. These suggestions are not a substitute for careful local planning but a survey of the possibilities from which choices can be made. They provide a skeleton that will need to be fleshed out according to the needs and capabilities of each worshiping community. For example, in the "green seasons" between Epiphany and Ash Wednesday and between Trinity Sunday and Advent, it may be appropriate in a given situation to use a general "Praise of God" hymn at the Entrance or a "Holy Communion" hymn at that point in the service rather than one of suggestions given here.

Although this listing has been compiled from the authorized hymnal of the Episcopal Church and its supplements published by Church Publishing, Inc., it has been created with the hope that it will also be useful in a larger ecumenical context. In that connection, it must be acknowledged that the quarter-century since the adoption of *The Hymnal 1982* has been a very fruitful one, both for the creation of new texts and tunes and for the compilation of new hymnals. As CPI's own publication of Michael Hudson's *Songs for the Cycle* (2004) attests, numerous writers have published collections of texts related to lectionary readings since the creation of H82. Some of these have been incorporated into the supplements indexed here, but there are many more to be explored. Also beyond what can be included here lies a wealth of settings that numerous composers have created for texts old and new.

One of the best ways to become acquainted with the broader ecumenical context from which the CPI supplements have been created is through The Hymn Society in the United States and Canada. A quick glance at the "Author and Composer Collections" section of their Book Service listings in any printed issue of *The Hymn* (or the online version at www.thehymnsociety.org/books) will show how many possibilities there are. In addition to these texts and tunes that have come out of North American and European contexts, there is an abundance of material coming from Africa, Asia, and the other Americas. Glimpses of this bounty can be seen from time to time in the materials indexed here, but the possibilities are constantly increasing. In a world that is becoming increasingly interdependent because of political and economic concerns, we need more than ever to affirm our connections with Christians around the globe by incorporating their sung prayer into our own.

Because this guide is specifically organized by the Revised Common Lectionary, the primary consideration for including hymns in the lists provided here has been their relationship to the appointed scripture passages. First priority has been given to metrical paraphrases or retellings of a passage, followed by texts that allude to portions of it. These directly-related texts are augmented by hymns that share a thematic emphasis or have some cultural association. Ordinarily a hymn is listed only once on a given day, but there are occasionally texts that allude to more than one appointed scripture and therefore appear more than once. Alternatively, hymns that are related to a specific day or season rather than to a specific scripture passage are listed before the lections and are marked [S]. This initial list also includes hymns related to the collect of the day [C] or the appointed psalm [P].

For each listed hymn, a suggestion is made for the place in the service where it is most likely to work well. In general, the beginning, middle, and end positions (Entrance, Offertory, and Postcommunion) are assigned for the more expansive, better-known, and more corporate hymns, while the more reflective, less-familiar, and more personal hymns are assigned to the positions framed by those positions (Sequence and Communion). A number of the hymns appointed for Communion, for example, have a refrain or some other feature than lends them to singing without reference to the printed page, making them appropriate for use while members of the congregation are moving. Also, because experience has shown that most worshipers make the connections between hymns and scripture better if they have heard the scripture first, it has been a general principle to have hymns follow rather than precede the scripture passages to which they are related. This pattern is not applied, however, to occasions in the church year when the emphasis of the day is already generally known (e.g. Christmas, Trinity Sunday, Thanksgiving Day).

In most cases, hymns are listed by the first line of the first stanza rather than by title or the first line of an opening refrain or antiphon, though there are occasions where exceptions have been made in order to use a well-known title or part of an identifying refrain. On the few occasions where metrical paraphrases of a relevant canticle (e.g. the Second Song of Isaiah) were not available, the canticle itself is suggested and is listed by first line rather than title.

In the two far-right columns following the hymn numbers are cross references to *The Crowning Glory: New Descants for Church Choirs* (CG descant) and *Trumpet Descants for 101 Noteworthy Hymns* (Inst desc) composed and arranged by Lorna Tedesco. Both resources are available from Church Publishing (www.churchpublishing.org) A shaded cell containing a circle ⊙ means that the hymn tune is available, but the text is not the same as hymn indicated. *Trumpet Descants* offers two descants in Bb for each hymn it contains. These descants may be played together or separately. In the organ score for the hymns these same descants appear in C and could be played by other instruments if desired.

In many ways, the present guide is a successor to the weekly Eucharistic listings of *A Liturgical Index to The Hymnal 1982* compiled by Marion J. Hatchett (CPI, 1986), which has helpfully informed what is presented here. Equally valuable has been his *Scriptural Index to The Hymnal 1982* (CPI, 1988), to which I am much indebted. Another great help in locating hymns related to passages not previously appointed has been *A Concordance of The Hymnal 1982* by Robert F. Klepper (Metuchen, NJ: Scarecrow Press, 1989). In addition I am grateful for the responses to preliminary versions of this guide from Carolyn Darr, SSM, Kevin R. Hackett, SSJE, Mark G. Meyer, and (by no means least) May B. Daw, as well as the encouragement from Marilyn Haskel and Frank L. Tedeschi of Church Publishing, Inc.

Carl P. Daw, Jr.

Carl P. Daw, Jr. is an Episcopal priest and writer who has served as the Executive Director of The Hymn Society in the United States and Canada since 1996. This ecumenical and international organization has its headquarters at Boston University School of Theology, where Dr. Daw serves as Adjunct Professor of Hymnology in the Master of Sacred Music program. He has been successively Secretary and Chair of the Standing Commission on Church Music of the Episcopal Church and was a consultant member of the Text Committee for *The Hymnal 1982*, to which he contributed a number of translations, metrical paraphrases, and original hymns. Four collections of his hymns have subsequently been published by Hope Publishing Co., and they have appeared in a wide range of denominational and ecumenical hymnals in the United States, Canada, England, Scotland, Australia, Hong Kong, and Japan as well as in several smaller collections and over sixty anthem settings. He was a member of the Editorial Advisory Committee for *The Hymnal 1982 Companion* and wrote the essay on "The Spirituality of Anglican Hymnody" in Volume I and numerous text commentaries in Volume III. Other Church Publishing, Inc. projects in which he has been involved include: *Breaking the Word: Essays on the Liturgical Dimensions of Preaching* (1994), for which he was the editor and a contributor of two essays, and (with Kevin R. Hackett, SSJE) *A HymnTune Psalter*, 2 vols. (1998-1999), now reissued in a Revised Common Lectionary edition (2007).

AN INTRODUCTION TO THE CHORAL ANTHEMS AND VOCAL SOLOS

The principals guiding the selection of hymns are paralleled in this compilation of choral anthems and vocal solos.

The anthems in this list represent over twelve years of hands-on parish worship planning according to the RCL, plus a concentrated six-month compilation specific to this resource. Considering the diversity represented in all of our churches, it is far from exhaustive. In completing this project in time for musicians to plan for Year A, time and space became major factors to which many good intentions had to be relinquished.

Time limited the ability to include much of the current output of living composers, and space limited us from listing all of the multiple settings of the most common scripture texts, Psalms and canticles. For example, the number of settings available to the text of the Magnificat is daunting, let alone the number of anthems and solos with the theme, "O Sing Unto the Lord."

The list includes many obvious choices, satisfying the needs of a first-year church musician utilizing this resource. It is our hope that it also includes selections that even seasoned musicians may have missed. The most important principal to keep in mind when perusing these pages is respecting your local tradition. Your own church or cathedral library is going to dictate how you will narrow your choices and apply them to your choirs. It is our intent that the settings listed here will not only serve as suggestions in themselves, but will also stir your creativity in applying similar choices that are already in your own choir's repertory.

As a practical budgetary consideration, many anthems appear multiple times, and, should you invest in a collection or major work included in these lists, you will find that many more than one movement or anthem are applicable throughout the year. Bach Cantatas and major works are included more for the potential of extracting choruses and solos than for their possible performance as a major work with orchestra. Most of the anthems are for adults, from simple unison/two-part to complex mixed/multi-part, and experienced trebles in unison/two-part. Vocal solos are also included, with a special emphasis during summer months.

My goal was to personally peruse all of the music in the lists with my own eyes, but as gaps appeared, and time raced by, I had to rely on trusted anthem lists with music by composers with a notable reputation. With time, these lists can expand to nearly limitless proportions.

It will be very apparent where the gaps lie in the availability of musical settings of scripture texts that are lesser known, and especially those which have only recently been introduced to the body of the lectionary. There is a plethora of texts in need of anthem and solo settings, providing all of us with the opportunity to narrow these gaps in the repertory by writing new textual paraphrases and new musical settings.

Choose wisely, and revel in the creative opportunities that lie ahead.

Thomas Pavlechko

Thomas Pavlechko has planned worship through four 3-year cycles of the Revised Common Lectionary. He is currently the Cantor and Composer in Residence at St. Martin's Lutheran Church in Austin, Texas. He served this church from 1994-2000 as Director of Music and Principal Organist, introducing the RCL in 1995. From 2000-2006, Pavlechko was the Organist-Choirmaster at Calvary Episcopal Church in Memphis, Tennessee, where he also introduced the RCL during its trial-use years in the Episcopal Church. Previously, he served as Organist-Choirmaster at St. Paul's Episcopal Church in Petersburg, Virginia, and All Saints Episcopal Church in Cincinnati, Ohio. Baptized a Lutheran and confirmed an Episcopalian, Pavlechko remains committed to both denominations.

A church musician for over twenty-nine years, Pavlechko has also been a member of the adjunct faculty at Richard Bland College of the College of William and Mary in Prince William, Virginia, and served as chapel musician, adjunct faculty, and liturgical consultant to the Lutheran Seminary Program in the Southwest, Austin. He recently held a seat on the Liturgical Music Editorial Team for the new hymnal of the Evangelical Lutheran Church in America.

Pavlechko is a published composer of choral anthems and service music settings, along with 84 hymns in print, and nearly 1,000 Psalm settings in three editions of St. Martin's Psalter. He was selected in 2002 as the Emerging Hymn Tune Composer by the Hymn Society, and his hymn tunes appear in hymnals in the United States, Canada and Australia. Pavlechko's music is published with Augsburg-Fortress, Church Publishing, E-Libris Publishers, GIA, Hope, Live Oak House, Selah and St. James Music Press.

SOURCES

Dimmock, Jonathan, "The Cantatas of J. S. Bach as Applied to the Revised Common Lectionary", available on the internet.

Jeffers, Ron, *Translations and Annotations of Choral Repertoire, Vol. I: Sacred Latin Texts*, © 1988, Earthsongs, 220 NW 29th St, Corvallis, Oregon 97330.

Jeffers, Ron and Gordon Paine, *Translations and Annotations of Choral Repertoire, Vol..II: German Texts*, © 2000, Earthsongs, 220 NW 29th St. Corvallis, Oregon 97330.

Laster, James H., *Catalogue of Choral Music Arranged in Biblical Order*, © 2001, Scarecrow Press Inc., www.scarecrowpress.com.

Laster, James H. and Strommen, Diana Reed, *Catalogue of Vocal Solos and Duets Arranged in Biblical Order*, © 2001, Scarecrow Press, Inc., www.scarecrowpress.com.

Setterlund, John S., *A Bach Lectionary*, 1995, brochure, 1305 Brian Place, Champaign, Illinois (217) 344-4654

Slonimnsky, Nicolas, *Baker's Biographical Dictionary of Musicians*, © 1992, Schirmer Books.

Stulken, Marilyn Kay and Seltz, Martin A., *Indexes for Worship Planning*, © 1996, Augsburg Fortress, www.augsburgfortress.org.

Wolff, Christoph , *The New Grove Bach Family*, © 1997, W. W. Norton & Co.

COMPOSERS OF MULTIPLE CHORALE, HYMN-BASED AND CHANT-BASED PRELUDES

Bach, Johann Sebastian
Bender, Jan
Bingham, Seth
Bolcom, William
Brahms, Johannes
Buxtehude, Dietrich
Cherwien, David
Darke, Harold
David, Johann Nepomuk
Distler, Hugo
Dupré, Marcel
Ferko, Frank
Gehring, Philip
Hancock, Gerre
Held, Wilbur
Hobby, Robert
Johnson, David
Krapf, Gerhard
Lenel, Ludwig
Manz, Paul
Near, Gerald

Ore, Charles
Pachelbel, Johann
Parry, Charles H. H.
Peeters, Flor
Pepping, Ernst
Pinkham, Daniel
Proulx, Richard
Read, Gardner
Reda, Siegfried
Scheidt, Samuel
Schroeder, Hermann
Schulz-Widmar, Russell
Sowerby, Leo
Stanford, Charles Villiers
Telemann, George Phillip
Vaughan Williams, Ralph
Walcha, Helmut
Walther, Johann
Willan, Healey
Wright, Searle
Wyton, Alec

COLLECTIONS OF CHORALE PRELUDES FOR ORGAN

Augsburg Organ Library: Advent, Christmas, Epiphany, Lent, Easter, Pentecost, November, Augsburg Fortress, www.augsburgfortress.org

Now Thank We All Our God, ed. C. H. Trevor, Oxford University Press, www.oup.co.uk/music

80 Chorale Preludes from the 17th and 18th Centuries, ed. Hermann Keller, Edition Peters, www.edition-peters.com/home.php.

TABLES

ANTHEM COLLECTIONS

16th	A Sixteenth-Century Anthem Book, Oxford University Press
100 CFC	100 Carols for Choirs, Oxford University Press
AFC 1	Anthems for Choirs 1, Oxford University Press
AFC 2	Anthems for Choirs 2, Oxford University Press
AFC 4	Anthems for Choirs 4, Oxford University Press
AUG	Augsburg Choirbook, Augsburg Fortress
BFAS	Bach for All Seasons, Augsburg Fortress
CFC 1	Carols for Choirs 1, Oxford University Press
CFC 2	Carols for Choirs 2, Oxford University Press
CHAN	Chantry Choirbook, Augsburg Fortress
CHES	Chester Books of Motets, Chester Music
CON	The Concord Anthem Book, E. C. Schirmer Music
NNOV	New Novello Anthem Book, Novello, London
OXCAB	Oxford Church Anthem Book, Oxford University Press
OXEA	The Oxford Easy Anthem Book, Oxford University Press
SEW	Sewanee Composers Project, St. James Press
TUD	Oxford Book of Tudor Anthems, Oxford University Press

COLLECTIONS OF VOCAL SOLOS

SOS	The Story of the Spirituals, compiled and arr. Boatner, McAfee Music Corp.
LIFT	Lift Up Your Voice
SS	The Sunday Solo

Anthem	Solo	Handbells	Voicing		Collection	Composer
				Isaiah 2:1-5		
X			unison	A Canticle of Peace		Joseph Clokey
X				And it Shall Come to Pass		Jean Berger
X				Christ Is the World's True Light	OXEA	W K Stanton
X				Judge Eternal		Gerre Hancock
X			Unison, 2 pt	Neath Vine and Fig Tree (Mic 4:1-4)		arr Hal H Hopson
				Psalm 122		
X				Behold Now, Bless the Lord (Ps 134)		Peter Hallock
X				I Rejoiced When I Heard Them Say		Richard Proulx
X				I Was Glad		Ronald Arnatt
X						William Boyce
X						Frank Ferko
X	X		2 pt			Peter Hallock
X			SSATTB			Charles H H Parry
X						Daniel Pinkham
X						Henry Purcell
X						Leo Sowerby
X				Jubilate Deo (Ps 100)		Multiple
X				Laetatus sum		Marc-Antonio Charpentier
X						Michael Haydn
X						Claudio Monteverdi
X				Let Us Go Rejoicing		Leon Roberts
X				O Be Joyful (Ps 100)		Multiple
X			unison	O Jerusalem		Malcolm Willliamson
X				O Pray for the Peace of Jerusalem		John Blow
X					AFC1	John Goss
X						Herbert Howells
X					16th	Thomas Tomkins
X				Peace Be within Thy Walls		Jean Berger
X				Pray for Peace		Alice Parker
X				Pray that Jerusalem May Have Peace		Charles V Stanford
X			TTBB or SSAA	The Gate of Heaven		Randall Thompson
				Romans 13:11-14		
X				Arise, Arise This Day Rejoice		Johann Walther
X				Christ Is the World's True Light	OXEA	W K Stanton
X				Out of Your Sleep	100CFC, CFC2	Richard R Bennett
X				Rejoice, O Jerusalem, Behold, Thy King		Healey Willan
X				The Night Is Far Spent		Knut Nystedt
X				Zion Hears the Watchman Singing	BFAS	harm J S Bach
X	X			Now It Is High Time, *Letters from St. Paul*		Daniel Pinkham
X				Nun komm der Heiden, *Cantata 61*		J S Bach
				Matthew 24:36-44		
X				Didn't It Rain		Carl MaultsBy
X				I Wanna Be Ready		James Miller
X				Lo! He Comes, With Clouds Descending		David H Williams
X			SATTB	My Lord, What a Morning		William Dawson
X	X			My Lord, What a Morning		Spiritual, Various
X				Out of Your Sleep	100CFC, CFC2	Richard R Bennett
X				Sleepers, Wake!	AFC1	Mendelssohn
X			SSATB	Therefore Watch that Ye Be Ready		Andreas Hammerschmidt
X				Watchman, Tell Us of the Night		Alan Hovhaness
X				Zion Hears the Watchman Singing	BFAS	harm J S Bach
X	X			Wachet auf ruft uns, *Cantata 140*		J S Bach
				Add'l Anthems, Cantatas, Major Works		
X				36: Schwingt freudig euch empor		J S Bach
X				62: Nun komm, der Heiden Heiland		J S Bach
X				90: Es reisset euch ein schrecklich Ende		J S Bach

Entrance	Sequence	Offertory	Communion	Postcommunion		H82	WLP	LEVAS II	VF	MHSO	CG descant	Inst descant
		X			Blest be the King whose coming [S]	74						X
			X		Once he came in blessing [S]	53						
X					The King shall come when morning dawns [S]	73						
					Isaiah 2:1-5							
	X				Christ is the world's true Light	542						X
		X			Come, we that love the Lord			12			X	
			X		Down by the riverside			210				
X					Glorious things of thee are spoken	522,523					X	
				X	Great day			5				
X		X		X	Judge eternal, throned in splendor	596						
	X				O day of God, draw nigh	600,601						
			X		Rockin' Jerusalem			17				
		X			Thy kingdom come, O God	613						
	X				"Thy kingdom come!" on bended knee	615						X
					Romans 13:11-14							
	X				Awake, my soul, and with the sun	11						
	X				Awake, my soul, stretch every nerve	546					X	
	X				Awake, thou Spirit of the watchmen	540						
			X		Better be ready			4				
		X			Eternal Ruler of the ceaseless round	617						
X					Hark! a thrilling voice is sounding	59						
	X				Stay awake, be ready					62		
					Matthew 24:36-44							
X		X		X	Jesus came, adored by angels	454						
X					Lo! he comes, with clouds descending	57,58					X	
			X		Rejoice! rejoice, believers	68					X	
				X	"Sleepers, wake!" A voice astounds us	61,62						

Anthem	Solo	Handbells	Voicing		Collection	Composer
				Isaiah 11:1-10		
				A Spotless Rose		Herbert Howells
				Be Peace on Earth	OXEA	William Crotch
			2 choirs	But these are they, *The Peaceable Kingdom*		Randall Thompson
				Fanfares		Daniel Pinkham
				How Bright Appears the Morning Star	BFAS	J S Bach
			Unison, fl	Isaiah's Song		Philip Baker
				Lo! How a Rose E'er Blooming		Hugo Distler
				O Day of Peace		Parry, arr Richard Proulx
				Peace in the Valley		Thomas A. Dorsey
			SATB or SAB	Song of the Advents		Russell Schulz-Widmar
			2 pt	There Shall Come Forth a Shoot from Jesse		Hal Hopson
				Virga Jesse floruit		Anton Bruckner
				Virga Jesse floruit, *Magnificat, Eb, BWV 243a*		J S Bach
				Psalm 72:1-7, 18-19		
				Blessed Be the Lord God		John Amner
						Daniel Moe
				Drop Down Ye Heavens	OXEA	Heathcote Statham
				He Delivered the Poor, *Hear My Words... People*		Charles H H Parry
				He Shall Come Down Like Rain		Dudley Buck
				Romans 15:4-13		
				Be Peace on Earth	OXEA	William Crotch
				Egre dictur virga		Jacob Handl
				Let All the People Praise Him		Lena McLin
				Lo How a Rose E'er Blooming		Hugo Distler
				May the God of Hope		Roberta Bitgood
				O Jesus, Grant Me Hope and Comfort		Johann Franck
				Savior of the Nations, Come	BFAS	J S Bach
				Thy King Cometh		Healey Willan
				Matthew 3:1-12		
				Be Peace on Earth	OXEA	William Crotch
				Comfort Ye		Gabriel Fauré
			2 pt	Make Straight in the Desert A Highway		Austin Lovelace
				Na Ioane Bapetiso-There was a man named John		Jacob Maka
				O Comfort Now My People	SEW	Thomas Pavlechko
				Prepare Ye the Way		Carl MaultsBy
				Prepare Ye the Way of the Lord		Michael Wise
			2 pt	The Kingdom of Love		David Ashley White
			Tenor	Comfort Ye, *Messiah*		G F Handel
			Tenor	Every Valley, *Messiah*		G F Handel
				Additional Music		
			Unison	Advent Message		Martin How
			SATB or 2 pt	An Advent Processional		Russell Schulz-Widmar
				Keep Your Lamps		André Thomas
				Cantatas/Major Works		
				61: Nun komm der Heiden Heiland		J S Bach
				62: Nun komm der Heiden Heiland		J S Bach

						H82	WLP	LEVAS II	VF	MHSO	CG descant	Inst descant
Entrance	Sequence	Offertory	Communion	Postcommunion								
■					Blessed be the God of Israel [S]	444						
■					Blessed be the God of Israel [S]		889					
					Hail to the Lord's Anointed [P]	616						■
					Isaiah 11:1-10							
			■		God is working his purpose out	534						■
	■	■			Isaiah the prophet has written of old		723					
		■			Lord, enthroned in heavenly splendor	307						
			■		O day of peace that dimly shines	597						
					Romans 15:4-13							
■					Holy Father, great Creator	368						■
			■		Redeemer of the nations, come	55						
					Savior of the nations, come	54						
					Matthew 3:1-12							
■		■			Christ is coming			6		58		
■					Comfort, comfort ye my people	67			32			
■					Hark! a thrilling voice is sounding	59						
■	■				Herald, sound the note of judgment	70						
■			■		On Jordan's bank the Baptist's cry	76						■
	■		■		Prepare the way, O Zion	65						
■					There's a voice in the wilderness crying	75						
			■		What is the crying at Jordan?	69					■	

Anthem	Solo	Handbells	Voicing		Collection	Composer
				Isaiah 35:1-10		
				And the Glory of the Lord, *Messiah*		G F Handel
				Bless the Lord, O My Soul	OXEA	C Armstrong Gibbs
				Comfort Ye, My People		George Thalben-Ball
				For All Flesh Is Like the Grass, *Requiem*		Johannes Brahms
				Look Toward the East		Thomas Pavlechko
				O Comfort Now My People	SEW	Thomas Pavlechko
				Song of Isaiah		Richard Proulx
				The Wilderness		John Goss
						Samuel Wesley
			Alto	Then Shall the Eyes..., *Messiah*		G F Handel
				Then Shall the Righteous Shine, *Elijah*		Felix Mendelssohn
				Psalm 146:4-9		
				Lauda anima mea Dominum		Orlando di Lasso
				My Soul, Sing the Praise of the Lord		Peter Hallock
				Psalm 146		Samuel Adler
						Jean Berger
						Peter Hallock
						Robert J Powell
						John Rutter
			Alto	Then Shall the Eyes..., *Messiah*		G F Handel
				Canticle (alt) Luke 1:46-55		
			SSA	Canticle of Mary		Libby Larsen
				Gospel Magnificat		Robert Ray
				Magnificat		Multiple
				The Mary Canticle		Leon Roberts
				James 5:7-10		
				Be Peace on Earth	OXEA	William Crotch
				Come Thou Long Expected Jesus	OXEA	Henry G Ley
				E'en So, Lord Jesus, Quickly Come		Paul Manz
				For All Flesh Is Like the Grass, *Requiem*		Johannes Brahms
			2 pt	God of Still Waiting		Alfred V Fedak
				O Rest in the Lord, *Elijah*		Felix Mendelssohn
				Matthew 11:2-11		
			SA	Behold, I Send My Messenger		Healey Willan
			3 pt or SATB	Go and Tell John		Lloyd Pfautsch
				O Comfort Now My People	SEW	Thomas Pavlechko
			Alto	O Thou That Tellest..., *Messiah*		G F Handel
				The Spirit of the Lord Is..., *The Apostles*		Edward Elgar
				Ärgre dich, o Seele, nicht, *Cantata 186*		J S Bach
				Prepare Thyself, Zion		J S Bach
			Alto	Then Shall the Eyes..., *Messiah*		G F Handel

Entrance	Sequence	Offertory	Communion	Postcommunion		H82	WLP	LEVAS II	VF	MHSO	CG descant	Inst descant
■					Blessed be the God of Israel [S]	444						
■					Blessed be the God of Israel [S]		889					
		■			Watchman, tell us of the night [S]	640					■	
					Isaiah 35:1-10							
	■				O for a thousand tongues to sing	493						■
	■				The desert shall rejoice		722					
					James 5:7-10							
■				■	Come, thou long-expected Jesus	66					O	
		■		■	O heavenly Word, eternal Light	63,64						
		■			The Lord will come and not be slow	462						
		■			"Thy kingdom come!" on bended knee	615						■
					Matthew 11:2-11							
■	■				Hark! the glad sound! the Savior comes	71,72						
■					Herald, sound the note of judgment	70						
	■				O for a thousand tongues to sing	493						■
■		■			On Jordan's bank the Baptist's cry	76						
■					Prepare the way, O Zion	65						
			■		Prepare the way of the Lord					61		
■					Prepare ye the way					63		
					Stay awake, be ready					62		
■					There's a voice in the wilderness crying	75						
				■	Word of God, come down on earth	633						

O Same tune, but not text   [S] Seasonal   [C] Collect   [P] Psalm   [GR] Gospel-related   [SC] Semi-continuous

Anthem	Solo	Handbells	Voicing		Collection	Composer
				Collect		
				The Best of Rooms		Randall Thompson
				Isaiah 7:10-16		
				Ecce concipies	CHES	Jacob Handl
				Ecce virgo concípiet	CHES	Heinrich Isaac
			SSATB			J P Sweelinck
				Wie shön leuchtet... , *Cantata 1*		J S Bach
			Alto	Behold, A Virgin Shall..., *Messiah*		G F Handel
				What You Goin' to Name the Baby?	SOS	Spiritual
				Psalm 80:1-7, 17-19		
				Advent Anthem		Richard Proulx
			SSAATB	Bread of Tears		Paul Christiansen
				From Thy Throne, O Lord		Richard Proulx
				Hear, O Thou Shepherd of Israel		William Mathias
				Romans 1:1-7		
				Come Thou Long Expected Jesus	OXEA	Henry G Ley
				E'en So, Lord Jesus, Quickly Come		Paul Manz
				Matthew 1:18-25		
				Ecce virgo concípiet	CHES	Heinrich Isaac
			SSATB			J P Sweelinck
				Jesu, dulcis memoria		Multiple
				Mary Had A Baby		arr. William Dawson
				Mary Was the Queen of Galilee		Wendall Whalum
			Sop	Now the Birth, *Hodie*		Ralph Vaughan Williams
			Alto	O Thou That Tellest, *Messiah*		G F Handel
				Savior of the Nations, Come	BFAS	J S Bach
				Song of Mary		Harold Friedell
			Alto	Behold, A Virgin Shall..., *Messiah*		G F Handel
			Tenor	Joseph, Thou Son of David, *Hodie*		Ralph Vaughan Williams
				What You Goin' to Name the Baby?	SOS	Spiritual
				Additional Music		
			2 pt treb or duet	I Sing of a Maiden		Bruce Neswick
			Unison or 4 pt	Mary Said Yes		Russell Schulz-Widmar
				Cantatas/Major Works		
				36: Schwingt freudig euch empor		J S Bach
				61: Nun komm der Heiden Heiland		J S Bach
				62: Nun komm der Heiden Heiland		J S Bach
				104: Du Hirte Israel, höre		J S Bach

Entrance	Sequence	Offertory	Communion	Postcommunion		H82	WLP	LEVAS II	VF	MHSO	CG descant	Inst descant
				■	God himself is with us [C]	475					■	
					Isaiah 7:10-16							
■		■			How bright appears the Morning Star	496,497						
			■	■	O come, O come, Emmanuel	56						■
					Romans 1:1-7							
■		■			Come, thou long-expected Jesus	66					○	
■					How bright appears the Morning Star	496,497						
					Matthew 1:18-25							
■					By the Creator, Joseph was appointed	261,262						
			■		Come now, and praise the humble saint	260						
				■	Creator of the stars of night	60						
■		■			How bright appears the Morning Star	496,497						
			■		Jesus, name above all names				81			
■					Mary, when the angel's voice				64			
			■	■	O come, O come, Emmanuel	56						■
■					Redeemer of the nations, come	55						
			■		Savior of the nations, come	54						
■					Stay awake, be ready					62		

Anthem	Solo	Handbells	Voicing		Collection	Composer
				Isaiah 9:2-7		
■				Dies sanctificatus		Multiple
■				For Unto Us a Child Is Born, *Messiah*		G F Handel
■				Puer natus est		Multiple
■				Unto Us Is Born A Son	100 CFC	arr David Willcocks
	■		Bass	The People That Walked..., *Messiah*		G F Handel
				Psalm 96		
■				Cantate Domino		Hans Leo Hassler
	■		opt str	O Sing Unto the Lord		Henry Purcell
■				O Sing Unto the Lord a New Song		Heinrich Schütz
■				The Beauty of Holiness		Kenneth Leighton
				Titus 2:11-14		
■				Bring Low Our Ancient Adam	BFAS	J S Bach
■				God Sent Forth His Son		Allen Orton Gibbs
				Luke 2:1-14 15-20		
■				Amen		Jester Hairston
■				Angelus ad pastores ait		Multiple
■				Der Engel sprach zu dem Hirten		Michael Praetorius
■				Gloria in excelsis		Multiple
■				Glory to God, *Messiah*		G F Handel
■				Mary Had a Baby		William Dawson
■				O, Bwana, U Tombee Sasa/Shout for Joy		Carl MaultsBy
■				Omnis mundus jocundetur		Michael Praetorius
■				Psallite		MichaelPraetorius
						Samuel Scheidt
■				Quem vidistis, pastores?		Multiple
■				Quempas Carol-Nunc Angelorum		Michael Praetorius
■				Resonet in laudibus		Multiple
■				The Virgin Mary Had a Baby		Jester Hairston
■				When God's Time Had Ripened		Alfred V Fedak
■				Cantata 191, Gloria in excelsis Deo		J S Bach
	■		Soprano	And There Were Shepherds, *Messiah*		G F Handel
	■		Soprano	And lo, the Angel of the Lord, *Messiah*		G F Handel
	■		Soprano	And the Angel Said..., *Messiah*		G F Handel
	■		Soprano	And Suddenly There Was..., *Messiah*		G F Handel
	■			Angel's Message..., *Christmas Story*		Heinrich Schütz
				Additional Music		
■			SSA	A Christmas Carol (What Sweeter Music)		Emma Lou Diemer
				All My Heart This Night Rejoices		Johann George Ebeling
				Betelehemu		Wendall Whalum
				Chorale Mass	BFAS	J S Bach
			SA, flute	Christmas Dance of the Shepherds		Zoltan Kodaly
				Christmas Spirituals		Joseph Joubert
		■	2 pt mixed	Divinum Mysterium		John Karl Hirten
				From Heaven Above to Earth...	BFAS	Johann Sebastian Bach
				Gloria, Gloria		David Hurd
				Hodie Christus natus est		Multiple
				O magnum mysterium		Multiple
			Unison	Three Moravian Carols		Phyllis Tate
			SATB or SAB	What Is This Lovely Fragrance		Gerald Near
				Cantatas/Major Works		
				63: Christen, ätzet diesen Tag		J S Bach
				91: Gelobet seist du, Jesu Christ		J S Bach
				110: Unser Mund sei voll Lachens		J S Bach
				248i: Jauchzet, frohlocket, auf,...		J S Bach
				Christmas Oratorio		J S Bach
				Gloria		Multiple

Entrance	Sequence	Offertory	Communion	Postcommunion		H82	WLP	LEVAS II	VF	MHSO	CG descant	Inst descant
					Isaiah 9:2-7							
	■			■	Hark! the herald angels sing	87						■
	■		■		It came upon the midnight clear	89,90						
				■	Sing, O sing, this blessed morn	88						
■	■				The people who in darkness walked	125,126					■	
■					Unto us a boy is born!	98						
					Titus 2:11-14							
	■				Joy to the world! the Lord is come	100					■	
					Luke 2:1-14 (15-20)							
■					A child is born in Bethlehem	103						
		■			A stable lamp is lighted	104						
		■			Angels we have heard on high	96					■	
			■		Away in a manger	101		27				
■					From heaven above to earth I come	80						
			■		Go, tell it on the mountain	99		21				
	■	■			God rest you merry, gentlemen	105						
		■			In the bleak midwinter	112						
		■			It came upon the midnight clear	89,90						
					Jesus our brother, kind and good					65		
		■			Lo, how a Rose e'er blooming	81						
					Mary borned a baby		22		37			
					Niño lindo / Child so lovely					69		
■	■				O come, all ye faithful	83						■
	■		■		O little town of Bethlehem	78,79						
■	■				Once in royal David's city	102			38			
					Shengye qing, shengye jing / Holy night, blessed night		725					
					Silent night, holy night	111		26				
					Star Child, earth Child				35			
					That boy-child of Mary was born in a stable			25		70		
		■			The first Nowell the angel did say	109						■
		■			The snow lay on the ground	110						

Anthem	Solo	Handbells	Voicing		Collection	Composer
				Isaiah 62:6-12		
■				Fanfares		Daniel Pinkham
■				Surely It Is God Who Saves Me		Jack Noble White
				Psalm 97		
■				This Lord Is King		Heinrich Schütz
				Titus 3:4-7		
■				All Who Believe and Are Baptized	BFAS	J S Bach
■				Salvation Has Come to Us		Johannes Brahms
■				Salvation Unto Us Has Come	BFAS	J S Bach
				Luke 2:(1-7) 8-20		
■				A Sound of Angels	AFC 1	Christopher Tye
■				Amen		Jester Hairston
■				Angelus ad pastores ait		Multiple
■				Der Engel sprach zu dem Hirten		Michael Praetorius
■				Gloria in excelsis		Multiple
■				Glory to God, *Messiah*		G F Handel
■				Mary Had a Baby		William Dawson
■				O, Bwana, U Tombee Sasa/Shout for Joy		Carl MaultsBy
■				O magnum mysterium		Multiple
■				Omnis mundus jocundetur		Michael Praetorius
■				Psallite		Michael Praetorius
■						Samuel Scheidt
■				Quem vidistis, pastores?		Multiple
■				Quempas Carol-Nunc Angelorum		Michael Praetorius
■				Resonet in laudibus		Multiple
■				The Virgin Mary Had a Baby		Jester Hairston
■				When God's Time Had Ripened		Alfred V Fedak
■				Cantata 191, Gloria in excelsis Deo		J S Bach
	■		Soprano	And There Were Shepherds, *Messiah*		G F Handel
	■		Soprano	And lo, the Angel of the Lord, *Messiah*		G F Handel
	■		Soprano	And the Angel Said..., *Messiah*		G F Handel
	■		Soprano	And Suddenly There Was..., *Messiah*		G F Handel
	■			Recit and Angel's Message..., *The Christmas Story*		Heinrich Schütz
				Cantatas/Major Works		
				63: Christen, ätzet diesen Tag		J S Bach
				91: Gelobet seist du, Jesu Christ		J S Bach
				110: Unser Mund sei voll Lachens		J S Bach
				248i: Jauchzet, frohlocket, auf,...		J S Bach
				Christmas Oratorio		J S Bach
				Gloria		Multiple

Entrance	Sequence	Offertory	Communion	Postcommunion		H82	WLP	LEVAS II	VF	MHSO	CG descant	Inst descant
					Isaiah 62:6-12							
	■				All you who love Jerusalem				157			
	■				Awake, thou Spirit of the watchmen	540						
	■				Surely it is God who saves me	678,679						
					Titus 3:4-7							
■		■		■	Good Christian friends, rejoice	107						■
			■		Love came down at Christmas	84						
					Luke 2:(1-7) 8-20							
	■	■			Angels we have heard on high	96					■	
■					Christians, awake, salute the happy morn	106						
			■	■	Go, tell it on the mountain	99	21					
■		■			O come, all ye faithful	83						■
■	■				Once in royal David's city	102			38			
		■		■	Hark! the herald angels sing	87						■
	■				There's a star in the east on Christmas morn			24				
			■	■	'Twas in the moon of wintertime	114						
	■			■	While shepherds watched their flocks by night	94,95						

Anthem	Solo	Handbells	Voicing		Collection	Composer
				Isaiah 52:7-10		
■				Break Forth Into Joy, *Messiah*		G F Handel
■				From Heaven Above to Earth I Come	BFAS	J S Bach
■				How Beauteous Are Their Feet		C V Stanford
			Soprano	How Beautiful Upon the Mountains	NNOV	John Stainer
				How Lovely Are the Messengers, *St. Paul*		Felix Mendelssohn
	■			How Beautiful Are the Feet, *Messiah*		G F Handel
				Psalm 98		
■				Cantate Domino		Multiple
■				Shout for Joy! Ps 100		John Carter
				Hebrews 1:1-4, 5-12		
■				Dies sanctificatus		Multiple
■				Let All the Angels of God, *Messiah*		G F Handel
■				Mirabile mysterium		Multiple
■				Of the Father's Heart Begotten	100 CFC, AFC 1	arr David Willcocks
	■		Tenor	Unto Which of the Angels, *Messiah*		G F Handel
				John 1:1-14		
■				Dies sanctificatus		Multiple
■				In dulci jubilo		Multiple
■				O admirabile commercium		Multiple
■			SATTB	O nata lux		William Byrd
■						William Mathias
■			SATTB			Thomas Tallis
	■		Alto	O Thou That Tellest, *Messiah*		G F Handel
			SA	The Word Was Made Flesh		Healey Willan
■				Thou Wilt Keep Him in Perfect Peace		Samuel Wesley
■				Verbum caro factum est		Multiple
■				When God's Time Had Ripened		Alfred V Fedak
				Additional Music		
■				Christmas Day		Gustav Holst
■				Hodie Christus natus est		Multiple
■				Song 46 (Christmas Day)		Orlando Gibbons
■				The Blessed Son of God, *Hodie*		Ralph Vaughan Williams
	■			Alfred Burt Carols		Alfred Burt
				Cantatas/Major Works		
				63: Christen, ätzet diesen Tag		J S Bach
				133: Ich freue mich in dir		J S Bach
				Christmas Oratorio, Part III, Cantata 248		J S Bach

Entrance	Sequence	Offertory	Communion	Postcommunion		H82	WLP	LEVAS II	VF	MHSO	CG descant	Inst descant
					Isaiah 52:7-10							
	▓				Watchman, tell us of the night	640					▓	
					Hebrews 1:1-4 (5-12)							
▓	▓				Angels, from the realms of glory	93						▓
	▓				Dost thou in a manger lie	97						
	▓				Now yield we thanks and praise	108						
▓		▓			Once in royal David's city	102			38			▓
		▓			The first Nowell the angel did say	109						▓
	▓				Where is this stupendous stranger?	491	726					
					John 1:1-14							
			▓		Father eternal, ruler of creation	573					▓	
			▓		From the dawning of creation		748					
▓			▓		Joy to the world! the Lord is come	100					▓	
		▓			Let all mortal flesh keep silence	324						▓
	▓				Listen, my friends					68		
	▓		▓		Love came down at Christmas	84						
		▓			O Savior of our fallen race	85,86						
	▓				Of the Father's love begotten	82						
▓					On this day earth shall ring	92						
	▓				Sing, O sing, this blessed morn	88						
			▓		What child is this, who, laid to rest	115						

▓ Same tune, but not text   [S] Seasonal   [C] Collect   [P] Psalm   [GR] Gospel-related   [SC] Semi-continuous

Anthem	Solo	Handbells	Voicing		Collection	Composer
				Isaiah 61:10—62:3		
				Arise, Shine, for Thy Light Has Come		Healey Willan
						Joel Martinson
				I Will Greatly Rejoice		Knut Nystedt
				The Spirit of the Lord is..., *The Apostles*		Edward Elgar
				I Will Greatly Rejoice in the Lord		Philip Young
				Psalm 147 or 147:13-21		
				Laudate Dominum		Multiple
				O Praise the Lord for It Is a Good Thing		Leo Sowerby
				Galatians 3:23-25; 4:4-7		
				All Who Believe and Are Baptized		J S Bach BFAS
				Bring Low Our Ancient Adam		J S Bach BFAS
				Of the Father's Heart Begotten	100 CFC, AFC 1	arr David Willcocks
				Salvation Has Come To Us		Johannes Brahms
				Salvation Unto Us Has Come	BFAS	J S Bach
				John 1:1-18		
				Dies sanctificatus		Multiple
				In dulci jubilo		Multiple
				Holy Is the True Light		William Harris
				Jesu, Joy—My Joy Forever	BFAS	J S Bach
				Mirabile mysterium		Multiple
				O admirabile commercium		Multiple
				O nata lux		Multiple
			Alto	O Thou That Tellest, *Messiah*		G F Handel
				Of the Father's Heart Begotten	100 CFC, AFC 1	arr David Willcocks
			SA	The Word Was Made Flesh		Healey Willan
				Thou Wilt Keep Him in Perfect Peace		Samuel Wesley
				Verbum caro factum est		Multiple
				When God's Time Had Ripened		Alfred V Fedak
				Additional Music		
				The Blessed Son of God, *Hodie*		Ralph Vaughan Williams
				Cantatas/Major Works		
				41: Jesu, nun sei gepreiset		J S Bach
				63: Christen, ätzet diesen Tag		J S Bach
				122: Das neugeborne Kindelein		J S Bach
				133: Ich freue mich in dir		J S Bach
				171: Gott, wie dein Name, so ist auch		J S Bach
				Christmas Oratorio, Part III, Cantata 248		J S Bach

	Entrance	Sequence	Offertory	Communion	Postcommunion		H82	WLP	LEVAS II	VF	MHSO	CG descant	Inst descant
						Isaiah 61:10-62:3							
		▓				Arise and shine, the prophet sang				156		O	
						Arise, shine, for your light has come	S 223ff	883					
						Galatians 3:23-25; 4:4-7							
	▓		▓			How bright appears the Morning Star	496,497						
						John 1:1-18							
				▓		Father eternal, Ruler of creation	573					▓	
					▓	From the dawning of creation		748					
						Let all mortal flesh keep silence	324						▓
	▓					Listen, my friends					68		
		▓		▓		Of the Father's love begotten	82						
						Word of God, come down on earth	633						

Anthem	Solo	Handbells	Voicing		Collection	Composer
				Collect		
■			SAB	Jesus! Name of Wondrous Love		Everett Titcomb
				Numbers 6:22-27		
■				The Lord Bless You and Keep You		Peter Lutkin
■						John Rutter
				Psalm 8		
■				O Lord Our Governor		Healey Willan
				Galatians 4:4-7		
■			SATB divisi	Little Lamb		David Cherwien
■				The Lamb		John Tavener
				Philippians 2:5-11		
■				Adoramus te, Christe		Multiple
■				At the Name of Jesus		Ralph Vaughan Williams
■				Christus factus est		Multiple
■				Let Thy Hand..., *Coronation Anthem No 2*		G F Handel
■				Let This Mind Be in You		Lee Hoiby
				Luke 2:15-21		
■				Jesu, dulcis memoria		Multiple
■			SAB	Jesus! Name of Wondrous Love		Everett Titcomb
■				Laud Ye the Name..., *All Night Vigil*		Sergei Rachmaninoff
■				Non nobis, Domine		Multiple
■				O admirabile commercium		Multiple
■				Quem vidistis, pastores?		Multiple
■				Resonet in laudibus		Multiple
	■			I Just Came from the Fountain	SOS	Spiritual
■				O Jesu, Name Most Lovely, *3 Short Sacred*		Heinrich Schütz
■				O Most Kind and Most Merciful Jesu		Heinrich Schütz
	■			What You Goin' to Name the Baby?	SOS	Spiritual
				Cantatas/Major Works		
				16: Herr Gott, dich loben wir		J S Bach
				28: Gottlob! nun geht das Jahr zu Ende		J S Bach
				41: Jesu, nun sei gepreiset		J S Bach
				143: Lobe den Herrn, meine Seele		attr. J S Bach
				171: Gott, wie dein Name, so ist auch...		J S Bach
				190: Singet dem Herrn ein neues Lied!		J S Bach
				Christmas Oratorio Cantata 248iv, Fallt...		J S Bach
				Das neugeborne Kindelein, BuxWV 13		Dietrich Buxtehude

						H82	WLP	LEVAS II	VF	MHSO	CG descant	Inst descant
				▨	Blessed be the Name [S]			78				
					Glorious is the Name of Jesus [S]			63				
					Jesus, name above all names [S]				81			
					Jesus, the very thought of thee [S]	642						
					How sweet the Name of Jesus sounds [S]	644						
				▨	Now greet the swiftly changing year [S]	250						
▨		▨		▨	O for a thousand tongues to sing [S]	493						▨
		▨			The Virgin Mary had a baby boy [S]					67		
		▨			There is a name I love to hear [S]			95				
		▨			There's something about that Name [S]			107				
		▨	▨		To the Name of our salvation [S]	248,249						
					Numbers 6:22-27							
				▨	God be with you			234				
					God be with you till we meet again		801					
			▨		May the Lord bless us					56		
				▨	The Lord bless you and keep you			231				
					Galatians 4:4-7							
	▨				Sing praise to our Creator	295						
					You're called by name, forever loved		766					
					Philippians 2:5-11							
			▨		A stable lamp is lighted	104						
▨		▨			All hail the power of Jesus' Name!	450,451						▨
					All praise to thee, for thou, O King divine	477						
					At the name of Jesus	435				135	▨	
	▨				From east to west, from shore to shore	77						
					Luke 2:15-21							
			▨		Jesus, name above all names				81			
					Jesus! Name of wondrous Love!	252						

Anthem	Solo	Handbells	Voicing		Collection	Composer
				Jeremiah 31:7-14		
■				For I Went with the Multitude	NNOV	Peter Aston
■				O, Bwana, U Tombee Sasa/Shout for Joy		Carl MaultsBy
■				Tomorrow Shall Be My Dancing Day		Multiple
	■		Alto	He Shall Feed His Flock, *Messiah*		G F Handel
				Psalm 84:1-8 9-12		
■				Behold, O God, Our Defender		Herbert Howells
■				How Lovely Is Thy Dwelling Place (Requiem)		Johannes Brahms
			SSAATTBB	Lord God of Hosts, How Lovely		Leland Sateren
■				O How Amiable		John Gardner
						Thomas Weelkes
■						Ralph Vaughan Williams
■				Quam Dilecta!		Kenneth Leighton
■						Charles-Marie Widor
	■		Contralto	Gott, der Herr, ist Sonn...*Cantata 79*		J S Bach
				Ephesians 1:3-6, 15-19a		
■				Blessed be the Father		Paul Christiansen
				Matthew 2:13-15, 19-23		
■				Of the Father's Love Begotten	100 CFC	arr David Willcocks
■				Puer natus est		Multiple
■				The Blessed Son of God, *Hodie*		Ralph Vaughan Williams
■				Unto Us Is Born a Son	100 CFC	arr David Willcocks
	■		Sop/Bass	Ach Gott, wie manches...*Cantata 58*		J S Bach
	■		Alto/Ten/Bass	Schau, lieber Gott..., *Cantata 153*		J S Bach
				Luke 2:41-52 alt		
■				My Son, Wherefore Hast Thou Done...		Heinrich Schütz
■				Liebster Jesu..., *Cantata 32*		J S Bach
■				Mein liebster Jesus..., *Cantata 154*		J S Bach
				Matthew 2:1-12 alt		
■				Kings to Thy Rising		Frank C Butcher
■				Magi veniunt ab oriente	CHES	Clemens non Papa
■				Omnes de Saba		Multiple
■				Reges terrae	CHES	Jean Mouton
■				The Three Kings	100 CFC	Peter Cornelius
■				Tribus miraculis	CHES	Luca Marenzio
■				Viderunt omnes		Multiple
■				Sie werden aus Saba..., *Cantata 65*		J S Bach
■				Ehre sei dir, Gott..., *Christmas Oratorio*		J S Bach
■				Herr, wenn die..., *Christmas Oratorio*		J S Bach
				Additional Music		
■				Children, Go Where I Send Thee		Mark Hayes
■				Jubilate Deo (Ps 100)		Multiple
■				O Be Joyful (Ps 100)		Multiple
				Cantatas/Major Works		
				124: Meinen Jesum lass ich nicht		J S Bach
				Das neugeborne Kindelein, BuxWV 13		Dietrich Buxtehude

Entrance	Sequence	Offertory	Communion	Postcommunion		H82	WLP	LEVAS II	VF	MHSO	CG descant	Inst descant
■				■	How bright appears the Morning Star [C]	496,497						
		■			How lovely is thy dwelling-place [P]	517					■	
■					Once in royal David's city [C]	102			38			
					Jeremiah 31:7-14							
	■				O God of Bethel, by whose hand	709					■	■
					Ephesians 1:3-6, 15-19a							
	■				In your mercy, Lord, you called me	706						
					Sing praise to our Creator	295						
					Matthew 2:13-15,19-23							
			■		Duérmete, Niño lindo/Oh, sleep now, holy baby	113						
					In Bethlehem a newborn boy	246						
					Lully, lullay, thou little tiny child	247						
		■			On this day earth shall ring	92						
■					Unto us a boy is born!	98						
					Luke 2:41-52							
			■		Our Father, by whose Name	587						
					When Jesus left his Father's throne	480						
					Matthew 2:1-12							
		■			As with gladness men of old	119						■
■					Brightest and best of the stars of the morning	117,118					■	
			■		Duérmete, Niño lindo/Oh, sleep now, holy baby	113						
■					Earth has many a noble city	127					■	
		■			Father eternal, Ruler of creation	573					■	
				■	Los magos que llegaron a Belén / The magi who to Bethlehem did go					71		
			■		On this day earth shall ring	92						
	■				Unto us a boy is born!	98						
■					The first Nowell the angel did say	109						■
		■			We three kings of Orient are	128						
	■				What star is this, with beams so bright	124						
					Where is this stupendous stranger?	491	726					
				■	Who are these eastern strangers?					72		

■ Same tune, but not text   [S] Seasonal   [C] Collect   [P] Psalm   [GR] Gospel-related   [SC] Semi-continuous

Anthem	Solo	Handbells	Voicing		Collection	Composer
				Collect		
	■			O God, Who By the Leading of a Star	AFC 1	Thomas Attwood
				Isaiah 60:1-6		
■			SSA	Arise, Shine		Charles Callahan
■			SAB, 2 inst			Marty Haugen
■				Arise, Shine, for Thy Light Is Come		Joel Martinson
■						William Mathias
■						Healey Willan
■				Dies sanctificatus		Multiple
■				In dulci jubilo		Multiple
■				Kings To Thy Rising		Frank C Butcher
■				O nata lux		Multiple
	■		Alto	O Thou That Tellest, *Messiah*		G F Handel
■				Omnes de Saba		Multiple
■				Surge illuminare		William Byrd
	■		Bass	For Behold, Darkness, *Messiah*		G F Handel
				Psalm 72:1-7, 10-14		
■				Drop Down, Ye Heavens	OXEA	Heathcote Statham
■				Omnes de Saba		Multiple
■	■			The Three Kings	100 CFC	Peter Cornelius
■				Tribus miraculis	CHES	Luca Marenzio
■				Viderunt omnes		Multiple
				Ephesians 3:1-12		
■				O magnum mysterium		Multiple
				Matthew 2:1-12		
■				Ballad of the Brown Kings		Margaret Bonds
■				Betelehemu		Wendell Whalum
■				Go Back Another Way		Glenn Burleigh
■				Kings To Thy Rising		Frank C Butcher
■			SSA	Lo, the Star Which They Saw		Healey Willan
■				Magi véniunt ab oriente	CHES	Clemens non Papa
■				Omnes de Saba		Multiple
■				Reges terrae	CHES	Jean Mouton
■	■			The Three Kings	100 CFC	Peter Cornelius
■				We Have Seen His Star		David Hurd
■				Viderunt omnes		Multiple
■				Sie werden aus Saba..., *Cantata 65*		J S Bach
■				Ehre sei dir, Gott..., *Christmas Oratorio*		J S Bach
■				Herr, wenn die stolzen ..., *Christmas Oratorio*		J S Bach
				Additional Music		
■				Break Forth O Beauteous	BFAS	J S Bach
■			SAB	Jesu, Bright and Morning Star		Leo Sowerby
■				O Morning Star, How Fair and Bright	BFAS	J S Bach
■				Once As I Remember	100 CFC	arr Charles Wood
		■		Man, the Child of God	LIFT	Hugo Wolf
				Cantatas/Major Works		
				123: Liebster Immanuel, Herzog der...		J S Bach

Entrance	Sequence	Offertory	Communion	Postcommunion		H82	WLP	LEVAS II	VF	MHSO	CG descant	Inst descant
■		■			Hail to the Lord's Anointed [P]	616						■
				■	How bright appears the Morning Star [S]	496,497						
		■			Now the silence [S]	333						
					Isaiah 60:1-6							
	■				Arise and shine, the prophet sang				156		o	■
	■				Arise, shine, for your light has come	S223ff	883					
	■				O very God of very God	672						
	■				O Zion, tune thy voice	543						
					Ephesians 3:1-12							
			■		Now, my tongue, the mystery telling	329,331						
	■				Our God, to whom we turn	681						
					Matthew 2:1-12							
■		■	■		As with gladness men of old	119						■
		■			Brightest and best of the stars of the morning	117,118					■	
			■		Duérmete, Niño lindo / Oh, sleep now, holy baby	113						
■	■		■		Earth has many a noble city	127					■	■
	■		■		Father eternal, Ruler of creation	573						■
		■			Los magos que llegaron a Belén / The magi who to Bethlehem did go					71		
			■		On this day earth shall ring	92						
	■				Songs of thankfulness and praise	135						■
	■				Unto us a boy is born!	98						
■	■				The first Nowell the angel did say	109						■
■		■			We three kings of Orient are	128						■
■		■			What star is this, with beams so bright	124						
	■				When Christ's appearing was made known (1,2,5)	131,132						
			■		Where is this stupendous stranger?	491	726					
			■		Who are these eastern strangers?					72		

Anthem	Solo	Handbells	Voicing		Collection	Composer
				Isaiah 42:1-9		
				Bless the Lord O My Soul	OXEA	C Armstrong Gibbs
				Hold Out Your Light		Lena McLin
				The Spirit of the Lord..., *The Apostles*		Edward Elgar
				This Little Light of Mine		John Work
				Psalm 29		
				Exaltabo te		Orlando di Lasso
			SSATB	Exaltabo te, Domine		G P Palestrina
				Give Unto the Lord		Edward Elgar
			SAB			Samuel Wesley
				Psalm 29		Heinrich Schütz
			SSATB			J P Sweelinck
			Unison			Jane Marshall
				Give God, the Father, Praise		Heinrich Schütz
				Acts 10:34-43		
				I Wonder As I Wander	100 CFC	arr John Rutter
				Joys Seven	100 CFC	arr Stephen Cleobury
				Lord of the Dance		arr John Ferguson
					100 CFC	arr David Willcocks
				Matthew 3:13-17		
				Come to the River		Mark Hayes
				Of the Father's Heart Begotten	100 CFC, AFC 1	arr David Willcocks
				The Blessed Son of God, *Hodie*		Ralph Vaughan Williams
				The Only Son From Heaven	BFAS	J S Bach
				This Is My Beloved Son		Knut Nystedt
				Tribus miráculis	CHES	Luca Marenzio
				Christ unser Herr zum..., *Cantata 7*		J S Bach
				Additional Music		
				Asperges me, Domine		Multiple
			2 voices	Vidi aquam - I Saw Water		David Hurd
			Unison	Loving Jesus, Gentle Lamb		Richard DeLong

	Entrance	Sequence	Offertory	Communion	Postcommunion		H82	WLP	LEVAS II	VF	MHSO	CG descant	Inst descant
	■					Songs of thankfulness and praise [S]	135						■
				■		Take me to the water [C]			134				
						Isaiah 42:1-9							
	■	■				Blessed be the God of Israel	444						
	■					Blessed be the God of Israel		889					
	■					Thy strong word did cleave the darkness	381						■
						Acts 10:34-43							
	■					In Christ there is no East or West	529		62			■	
						Matthew 3:13-17							
			■			Christ, when for us you were baptized	121						
		■				From God Christ's deity came forth	443						
			■			"I come," the great Redeemer cries	116						
	■	■			■	O love, how deep, how broad, how high(1-3,6)	448,449					■	
						The sinless one to Jordan came	120					■	
	■					When Christ's appearing was made known (1,3,5)	131,132						
		■				When Jesus went to Jordan's stream	139						

Anthem	Solo	Handbells	Voicing		Collection	Composer
				Collect		
				Christ Is the World's True Light	OXEA	W K Stanton
				O Almighty God	AFC 1	George Barcrofte
				Isaiah 49:1-7		
				Christ, Whose Glory Fills the Skies	OXCAB	Thomas Armstrong
						T Frederick Candlyn
				Sing, O Heavens		Emma Lou Diemer
				This Little Light of Mine		John Work
				Hear Ye, Israel, *Elijah*		Felix Mendelssohn
				Psalm 40:1-12		
				Give Ear Unto My Prayer		Jacques Arcadelt
			SATB & SA	I Waited for the Lord, *Hymn of Praise*		Felix Mendelssohn
			2-pt treble	I Waited Patiently for the Lord		Ronald Arnatt
				Psalm 40		Samuel Adler
				Thy Law Is Within My Heart		Robert Powell
				Wait on the Lord, *The Coming*		Leon Roberts
				With Quiet Calm Forbearing		Heinrich Schütz
				O Rest in the Lord, *Elijah*		Felix Mendelssohn
				I Corinthians 1:1-9		
				Draw Us in the Spirit's Tether		Harold Friedell
				God Is Faithful		Walter Pelz
			2 pt or SATB	God Make You Blameless		Thomas Gieschen
			Alto	Gott soll allein mein…, *Cantata 169*		J S Bach
				John 1:29-42		
				Agnus Dei		Multiple
			SA	Behold the Lamb of God		Paul Bouman
						Karl Graun
						Healey Willan
				Behold the Lamb of God, *Messiah*		G F Handel
				I Believe That This Is Jesus!		Undine Smith Moore
				Little Lamb		David Cherwien
				The Lamb		John Tavener
				These Are They Which Follow the Lamb	AFC 1	John Goss
				Tu es Petrus		Maurice Duruflé
			SATB/B solo			Gabriel Fauré
						Hans Leo Hassler
						Claudio Monteverdi
						G P Palestrina
						Charles-Marie Widor
				Wondrous Love		Various
				Cantatas/Major Works		
				9: Es ist das Heil uns kommen her		J S Bach

Entrance	Sequence	Offertory	Communion	Postcommunion		H82	WLP	LEVAS II	VF	MHSO	CG descant	Inst descant
				X	Christ is the world's true Light [C]	542						
			X		The light of Christ [C]					80		
					Isaiah 49:1-7							
X					Christ, whose glory fills the skies	6,7						X
	X				God of mercy, God of grace	538						
X					How wondrous and great thy works, God of praise!	532,533						X
	X				O Zion, tune thy voice	543						
					1 Corinthians 1:1-9							
X			X		I am the church! You are the church!					109		
			X		Strengthen for service, Lord, the hands	312						
X			X		We the Lord's people, heart and voice uniting	51					X	
					John 1:29-42							
	X			X	By all your saints still striving (St. Andrew)	231,232					X	
					I have decided to follow Jesus			136				
					In your mercy, Lord, you called me	706						
		X		X	Jesus calls us; o'er the tumult	549,550			128,129			X
			X		Lord, enthroned in heavenly splendor	307						
				X	What does it mean to follow Jesus?					89		
			X		What wondrous love is this	439						X
				X	Will you come and follow me		757					
				X	Ye servants of God, your Master proclaim	535						X

Same tune, but not text   [S] Seasonal   [C] Collect   [P] Psalm   [GR] Gospel-related   [SC] Semi-continuous

Anthem	Solo	Handbells	Voicing		Collection	Composer
				Collect		
■				Almighty and Everlasting God	TUD	Orlando Gibbons
				Isaiah 9:1-4		
■				Arise, Shine, for Thy Light Is Come		Joel Martinson
						William Mathias
						Healey Willan
■				His Yoke Is Easy, *Messiah*		G F Handel
	■		Alto/Sop	He Shall Feed /Come Unto Him, *Messiah*		G F Handel
	■		Bass	The People That Walked..., *Messiah*		G F Handel
				Psalm 27:1, 5-13		
■				Arise, Shine, for Thy Light Is Come		Joel Martinson
						William Mathias
						Healey Willan
■			SAB	God Is My Strong Salvation		Robert J Powell
				Hide Not Thou Thy Face		Richard Farrant
				Jesus Lover of..., *Playing Gospel Piano*		Edwin Hawkins
	■			Nobody Knows the Trouble I've Seen		Spiritual, Various
				One Thing Have I Desired		Herbert Howells
				One Thing I Seek		Robert Hobby
				The Lord Is My Light		Peter Hallock
				The Lord Is My Light and My Salvation		John Rutter
						Stephen Sturk
				Thou Knowest, Lord, the Secrets...		Henry Purcell
				I Corinthians 1:10-18		
■			Unison	Three Gifts – Faith, Hope, Love		Pauline Delmonte
				Ubi caritas		Maurice Duruflé
				Matthew 4:12-23		
■				All the Way		James Bignon
■				Arise, Shine, for Thy Light Is Come		Joel Martinson
						William Mathias
						Healey Willan
				Dear Lord and Father of Mankind		Charles H H Parry
				Dies sanctificatus		Multiple
				How Lovely Are the Messengers, *St. Paul*		Felix Mendelssohn
				I Believe That This Is Jesus!		Undine Smith Moore
				O nata lux		Multiple
				The Fisherfolk		Betty Carr Pulkingham
	■		Bass	The People That Walked..., *Messiah*		G F Handel
				Additional Music		
■				Christ Is the World's True Light	OXEA	W K Stanton
			SAB	Jesu, Bright and Morning Star, SAB		Leo Sowerby
				O factura Dei, *The Hildegard Motets*		Frank Ferko
				Lobet den Herrn alle Heiden		J S Bach

Entrance	Sequence	Offertory	Communion	Postcommunion		H82	WLP	LEVAS II	VF	MHSO	CG descant	Inst descant
			■		As we gather at your Table [C]		763				O	
■		■			How wondrous and great thy works, God of praise! [C]	532,533						■
			■		My God, thy table now is spread [C]	321					■	
				■	Spread, O spread, thou mighty word [C]	530						
					Isaiah 9:1-4							
		■			Singing songs of expectation	527						■
■	■				The people who in darkness walked	125,126						■
■					Thy strong word did cleave the darkness	381						
					1 Corinthians 1:10-18							
			■		God is Love, and where true love is	576,577						■
		■	■		I come with joy to meet my Lord	304						■
			■		Ubi caritas et amor		831					
■			■		Where charity and love prevail	581						
			■		Where true charity and love dwell	606						
					Matthew 4:12-23							
	■				Jesus calls us, o'er the tumult	549,550			128,129			■
		■			Put down your nets and follow me		807					
		■			They cast their nets in Galilee	661						
		■			Tú has venido a la orilla / You have come down to the lakeshore		758					
		■			When Jesus saw the fishermen					76		
		■			Will you come and follow me		757					

Anthem	Solo	Handbells	Voicing		Collection	Composer
				Micah 6:1-8		
			Unison	God's Requirements		Samuel Adler
				The Twin Commandments		Jane Marshall
				Walk Humbly with Thy God		Handel, arr Carl Fredrickson
						Carl Mueller
				With What Shall I Come Before the Lord?		Jane Marshall
				Psalm 15		
				Lord, Who Shall Abide		Glenn W Darst
				Lord, Who Shall Abide in Thy Tabernacle?		Arthur Bliss
				Lord, Who Shall Abide in Thy Temple, *Four Motets*		Alan Hovhaness
			SAB, guitar, fl	Who Shall Abide		Walter Pelz
				Who May Lodge in Thy Tabernacle?		Daniel Pinkham
				Who Shall Abide in Thy Tabernacle		G B Pergolesi
				I Corinthians 1:18-31		
				The Foolishness Carol		Austin Lovelace
				The Wisdom of God		Austin Lovelace
				Matthew 5:1-12		
				Beatitudes		Russian Chant
			2 pt	Blessed Are the Merciful		David H. Williams
				Blessed Are the Pure in Heart		Walford Davies
				Blessed Are Those Who Mourn, *Requiem*		Johannes Brahms
				Blessed Is the Man, *All Night Vigil*		Serge Rachmaninoff
				Exceeding Glad, *Coronation Anthem No. 3*		G F Handel
				For the Feast of All Saints		Gerald Near
				Let Nothing Ever Grieve Thee		Johannes Brahms
				Soon-Ah Will Be Done		arr William Dawson
				Swing Low, Sweet Chariot		arr Dale Adelmann
			2 pt treble	The Beatitudes		Jan Bender
				Cantatas/Major Works		
				107: Was willst du dich betrüben		J S Bach

Entrance	Sequence	Offertory	Communion	Postcommunion		H82	WLP	LEVAS II	VF	MHSO	CG descant	Inst descant
					God the Omnipotent! King, who ordainest [C]	569						
					Micah 6:1-8							
■		■			Before thy throne, O God, we kneel	574,575						■
■					What does the Lord require	605						
			■		What does the Lord require of you?					153		
					1 Corinthians 1:18-31							
	■				Cross of Jesus, cross of sorrow	160						
	■				In the cross of Christ I glory	441,442						
	■				Nature with open volume stands	434						
	■				The old rugged cross			38				
	■				We sing the praise of him who died	471						
					Matthew 5:1-12							
		■			Beati		828					
■	■				Blest Jesus, at thy word	440						
		■			Blest are the poor in spirit					74		
			■		Blest are the pure in heart	656						
		■	■		Gracious Spirit, give your servants		782					
			■		Lord, make us servants of your peace	593						
■			■		Rejoice, ye pure in heart	556,557						■
			■		Remember your servants, Lord	560						
			■		'Tis the gift to be simple	554						
			■		You shall cross the barren desert		811					

Anthem	Solo	Handbells	Voicing		Collection	Composer
				Isaiah 58:1-9a [9b-12]		
				Be Peace on Earth	OXEA	William Crotch
				He That Is Down Need Fear No Fall	OXEA	John Dowland
						Philip Moore
						Ralph Vaughan Williams
				His Yoke Is Easy, *Messiah*		G F Handel
				He Shall Feed.../Come Unto Him, *Messiah*		G F Handel
				Psalm 112:1-9 [10]		
				Beatus vir		G Carissimi
						W A Mozart
						Claudio Monteverdi
						Antonio Vivaldi
				Blessed Are the Men Who..., *Elijah*		Felix Mendelssohn
			SATB or SSAB	O Happy Man		Henry Purcell
				I Corinthians 2:1-12 [13-16]		
				Eye Hath Not Seen		Walter Wade
	2 pt			Oculus non vidit	AFC 2	Orlando di Lasso
				Matthew 5:13-20		
				If Ye Love Me		Thomas Tallis
						Philip Wilby
						Daniel Pinkham
						Healey Willan
				Lead Me, Lord		Samuel Wesley
				Light and Salt		Erik Routley
				This Little Light of Mine		Spiritual, Various
				Ye Are the Light of the World		Carl F Mueller
				Additional Music		
				Cantatas/Major Works		
				39: Brich dem Hungrigen dein Brot		J S Bach

Entrance	Sequence	Offertory	Communion	Postcommunion		H82	WLP	LEVAS II	VF	MHSO	CG descant	Inst descant
	▓			▓	The church of Christ in every age [C]		779				▓	
▓					Thy strong word did cleave the darkness [C]	381						▓
					Isaiah 58:1-9a (9b-12)							
	▓			▓	Gracious Spirit, give your servants		782				o	
	▓				Lord, whose love through humble service	610						
▓					Now quit your care (3-5)	145						
▓					O day of God, draw nigh	600,601						
					1 Corinthians 2:1-12 (13-16)							
▓			▓		Lord, speak to me, that I may speak				98			
			▓		There is a longing in our hearts, O Lord				147			
					Matthew 5:13-20							
		▓			Longing for light					59		
		▓			Lord, make us servants of your peace	593						
			▓		Out in the highways and byways of life (Make me a blessing)			158				
▓					Praise to the living God!	372					▓	
		▓			This little light of mine			160,221				
	▓		▓		We are marching in the light of God		787					

Anthem	Solo	Handbells	Voicing		Collection	Composer
				Deuteronomy 30:15-20		
				Blessed Are the Undefiled		Healey Willan
				Create in Me a Clean Heart		Paul Bouman
						Johannes Brahms
				Gloria in Excelsis, *All Night Vigil*		Sergei Rachmaninoff
				If Ye Love Me		Thomas Tallis
						Philip Wilby
				Miserere		Gregorio Allegri
				O For a Closer Walk with God	AFC 1	Charles V Stanford
				Teach Me, O Lord, the Way of Thy Statutes		Thomas Attwood
			SAATB			William Byrd
			SSATB			John Hilton
						David Hurd
			Unison, 2 pt			Knut Nystedt
				Sirach 15:15-20		
				Gloria in Excelsis, *All Night Vigil*		Sergei Rachmaninoff
				If Ye Love Me		Thomas Tallis
						Philip Wilby
						Daniel Pinkham
						Healey Willan
				O For a Closer Walk with God	AFC 1	Charles V Stanford
				Teach Me, O Lord, the Way of Thy Statutes		see above
				Psalm 119:1-8		
			SAATB	Ad Dominum cum tribularer		Hans Leo Hassler
				Beati immaculate		Tomas Victoria
				Beati quarum via		Charles V Stanford
			2 pt treble	Blessed Are the Undefiled		Healey Willan
			2 pt or SATB	Blessed Are Those		Maurice Greene
						Roger Petrich
						Thomas Tallis
				Gloria in excelsis, *All Night Vigil*		Sergei Rachmaninoff
				O For a Closer Walk with God	AFC 1	Charles V Stanford
			SATB/SATB	Prayer		Alice Parker
				Teach Me, O Lord, the Way of Thy Statutes		see above
				Unveil Mine Eyes		Robert J Powell
				I Corinthians 3:1-9		
				Be Peace on Earth		William Crotch
				For We Are Laborers Together With God	OXEA	Leo Sowerby
			2 pt	Temples of God		Ronald Nelson
				Ubi caritas		Maurice Duruflé
				Matthew 5:21-37		
				I Want Heaven to Be Mine		Moses Hogan
				If Ye Love Me		Daniel Pinkham
						Thomas Tallis
			SSA			Healey Willan
						Philip Wilby
				Judge Eternal		Gerre Hancock
				Lord, For Thy Tender Mercy's Sake		Richard Farrant
				Turn Back, O Man		Gustav Holst
				Ubi caritas		Maurice Duruflé
			Alto	Vergnügte Ruh', beliebte Seelenlust, *Cantata 170*		J S Bach
				Cantatas/Major Works		
				9: Es ist das Heil uns kommen her		J S Bach
				33: Allein zu dir, Herr Jesu Christ		J S Bach

						H82	WLP	LEVAS II	VF	MHSO	CG descant	Inst descant
Entrance	Sequence	Offertory	Communion	Postcommunion								
					If thou but trust in God to guide thee [C]	635						
					Deuteronomy 30:15-20							
					Come, gracious Spirit, heavenly Dove	512						
					God of grace and God of glory	594,595					■	
					Lord, be thy word my rule	626						
					Now that the daylight fills the skies	3,4						
					Praise to the living God	372						■
					Sirach 15:15-20							
					Come, Gracious Spirit, heavenly Dove	512						
					God of grace and God of glory	594,595					■	
					Lord, be thy word my rule	626						
					Now that daylight fills the skies	3,4						
					Praise to the living God	372						■
					1 Corinthians 3:1-9							
					Brother, sister, let me serve you				124	94		
					Come now, O Prince of peace		795					
					I come with joy to meet my Lord	304					■	
					Lord, make us servants of your peace	593						
					People of God, gather together				109			
					Ubi caritas et amor		831					
					We are all children of the Lord					105		
					Where charity and love prevail	581						
					Matthew 5:21-37							
					Blessed Jesus, at thy word	440						
					"Forgive our sins as we forgive"	674					■	
					Go forth for God; go to the world in peace	347						
					I will trust in the Lord			193				
					Strengthen for service, Lord	312						

Anthem	Solo	Handbells	Voicing		Collection	Composer
				Leviticus 19:1-2, 9-18		
				Holy holy		Richard Smallwood
				O Lord Most Holy		César Franck
				Psalm 119:33-40		
				Gloria in excelsis, *All Night Vigil*		Sergei Rachmaninoff
				I'm Waiting		Melvin Crispell
			Unison treble	O Turn Away Mine Eyes		William Boyce
				Teach Me, O Lord, the Way of Thy Statutes		Thomas Attwood
			SAATB			William Byrd
			SSATB			John Hilton
						David Hurd
			Unison, 2 pt			Knut Nystedt
				I Corinthians 3:10-11, 16-23		
				Behold the Tabernacle of God		William H Harris
				Christ Is Made the Sure Foundation		Dale Wood
				For We Are Laborers Together with God		Leo Sowerby
				The Best of Rooms		Randall Thompson
				The Church's One Foundation		M. Roger Holland
				Matthew 5:38-48		
				Beatitudes		Russian Chant
				Blessed Are the Pure in Heart		Walford Davies
				Blessed Are They That Mourn	OXCAB	Johannes Brahms
				Blessed Is the Man, *All Night Vigil*		Serge Rachmaninoff
			SATB, T solo	Grieve Not the Holy Spirit		T Tertius Noble
				Let Nothing Ever Grieve Thee		Johannes Brahms
				Cantatas/Major Works		
				138: Warum betrübst du dich, mein Herz?		J S Bach

						H82	WLP	LEVAS II	VF	MHSO	CG descant	Inst descant
					Love divine, all loves excelling [C]	657					▓	
					Leviticus 19:1-2,9-18							
	▓				For the fruit of all creation	424						
▓					Thy strong word did cleave the darkness	381						▓
					1 Corinthians 3:10-11, 16-23							
	▓				Blest are the pure in heart	656						
▓		▓			Christ is made the sure foundation	518					▓	
▓		▓			Creator Spirit, by whose aid	500						
▓			▓		How firm a foundation, ye saints of the Lord	636,637						
▓					The Church's one foundation	525					▓	
					Matthew 5:38-48							
			▓		As we gather at your Table		763				0	
			▓		Creating God, your fingers trace	394,395						
			▓		Go forth for God; go to the world in peace	347						
			▓		God of freedom, God of justice				90			
			▓		Jesu, Jesu, fill us with your love	602		74				
			▓		Lord, make us servants of your peace	593						
			▓		Lord, whose love through humble service	610						
			▓		Now that the daylight fills the sky	3,4						
			▓		O splendor of God's glory bright	5						
	▓		▓		When Christ was lifted from the earth	603						

Anthem	Solo	Handbells	Voicing		Collection	Composer
				Isaiah 49:8-16a		
■				Look Toward the East		Thomas Pavlechko
■				O Comfort Now My People	SEW	Thomas Pavlechko
■			SSAATBB	Sing O Heavens		John Amner
				The First Song of Isaiah		Jack Noble White
■			SSATB	Zion Said		Andreas Hammerschmidt
■			SSATB	Zion's Lament		Andreas Hammerschmidt
■			SSATB	Zion Speaks, I Am by God Forsaken		Johann H Schein
	■		Tenor	Comfort Ye, *Messiah*		G F Handel
	■		Tenor	Every Valley, *Messiah*		G F Handel
				Psalm 131		
■				Chichester Psalm No. III (Ps 133)		Leonard Bernstein
			SATB & SA	I Waited for the Lord, *Hymn of Praise*		Felix Mendelssohn
■				I Waited Patiently for the Lord		Ronald Arnatt
	■		Alto/Sop	He Shall Feed /Come Unto Him, *Messiah*		G F Handel
	■			O Rest in the Lord, *Elijah*		Felix Mendelssohn
				I Corinthians 4:1-5		
■				Thou Knowest, Lord, the Secrets of Our Hearts		Henry Purcell
				Matthew 6:24-34		
■				Jesu, Joy of Man's Desiring	BFAS	J S Bach
■				Jesu meine Freude	BFAS	J S Bach
■				Let Nothing Ever Grieve Thee		Johannes Brahms
■				Quaerite primum regnum Dei, Seek Ye First		W A Mozart
■			2 pt	Seek Ye First the Kingdom of God		Theron Kirk
■				Vox ultima crucis: Tarry No Longer	OXEA	William H Harris
■				Warum betrübst du dich, mein Herz?, *Cantata 138*		J S Bach
■				Fear Not, Little Flock, *Cantata 175*	LIFT	J S Bach
	■		Soprano	Jauchzet Gott in allen Landen!, *Cantata 51*		J S Bach
				Additional Music		
■			Unison, vln	I Trust in Thee, Lord Jesus		Bononcini, arr Swallow
■				In Thee, O Lord, Have I Trusted	CON	G F Handel
				Cantatas/Major Works		
				187: Es wartet alles auf dich		J S Bach
				Jesu, meine Freude, BWV 227 (motet)		J S Bach

	Entrance	Sequence	Offertory	Communion	Postcommunion		H82	WLP	LEVAS II	VF	MHSO	CG descant	Inst descant
Isaiah 49:8-16a													
		■				Through north and south and east and west		822					■
			■			Give praise and glory unto God	375						
		■				If thou but trust in God to guide thee	635						
				■		Loving Spirit, loving Spirit		742		51			
	■		■			O God of Bethel, by whose hand	709					■	
		■				O Zion, tune thy voice	543						■
	■					Praise to the Lord, the Almighty	390						■
			■			Sing praise to God who reigns above	408					o	
		■				Surely it is God who saves me	678,679						
1 Corinthians 4:1-5													
		■				O day of God, draw nigh	600,601						
						Put forth, O God, thy Spirit's might	521						
Matthew 6:24-34													
				■		By gracious powers so wonderfully sheltered	695,696					■	
				■		Commit thou all that grieves thee	669						■
				■		His eye is on the sparrow			191				■
				■		Jesus, all my gladness	701						
	■			■		Joyful, joyful, we adore thee	376						■
			■			Seek ye first the kingdom of God	711						■
			■			Sometimes a light surprises	667						

Anthem	Solo	Handbells	Voicing		Collection	Composer
				Exodus 24:12-18		
■				Changed		Walter Hawkins
■				Great and Glorious		F J Haydn
■				I to the Hills Lift Up Mine Eyes		Jean Berger
	■		Alto	O Thou That Tellest, *Messiah*		G F Handel
				Psalm 2		
■				Be Peace on Earth	OXEA	William Crotch
■				Dixit Dominus (Ps 110)		Multiple
■				Let Us Break Their Bonds, *Messiah*		G F Handel
■				Of the Father's Heart Begotten	100 CFC, AFC 1	arr David Willcocks
■				This Is My Beloved Son		Knut Nystedt
■				We Have Heard with Our Ears Ps. 44		Herbert Howells
	■		Tenor	He That Dwelleth in Heaven, *Messiah*		G F Handel
	■		Tenor	Thou Shalt Break Them, *Messiah*		G F Handel
			Bass	Why Do the Nations..., *Messiah*		G F Handel
				Psalm 99		
			SATB/SATB	Derr Herr ist König		Johann Pachelbel
				Dominus regnavit		Peter Hallock
				Let All Mortal Flesh Keep Silence		Edward Bairstow
						Gustav Holst
■				Sanctus		Multiple
				2 Peter 1:16-21		
■				Christ Is the World's True Light	OXEA	W K Stanton
■				Christ, Whose Glory Fills the Skies	OXCAB	Thomas Armstrong
						T Frederick Candlyn
■				Every Time I Feel the Spirit		arr William Dawson
■			SAB or SSA	Lord, You Know I Been Changed		Carl MaultsBy
■				The Only Son from Heaven	BFAS	J S Bach
■				This Is My Beloved Son		Knut Nystedt
■				Worthy Is the Lord		William Murphy Jr & Shannon Davis
				Matthew 17:1-9		
■				Beautiful Savior		F Melius Christiansen
■				Changed		Walter Hawkins
■				Christ, Whose Glory Fills the Skies	OXCAB	Thomas Armstrong
						T Frederick Candlyn
	■		SAB	Fairest Lord Jesus		Russell Schulz-Widmar
			SAB or SSA	Lord, You Know I Been Changed		Carl MaultsBy
				O nata lux		William Byrd
						William Mathias
						Thomas Tallis
	■		Alto	O Thou That Tellest, *Messiah*		G F Handel
				The Spirit of The Lord..., *The Apostles*		Edward Elgar
				This Is My Beloved Son		Knut Nystedt
				Of the Father's Heart Begotten	100 CFC, AFC 1	arr David Willcocks
				Additional Music		
■				Alleluia		Multiple
■				O Morning Star How Fair and Bright	BFAS	J S Bach
■				Te Deum		Multiple
■				The Heavens Are Telling		G F Handel
						F J Haydn
				Cantatas/Major Works		
				130: Herr Gott, dich loben alle wir		J S Bach

						H82	WLP	LEVAS II	VF	MHSO	CG descant	Inst descant
■		■		■	Songs of thankfulness and praise [S]	135						■
				■	Alleluia, song of gladness [S]	122,123						
					Exodus 24:12-18							
■					We sing of God, the mighty source of all things	386,387						
					2 Peter 1:16-21							
■				■	Christ is the world's true Light	542						■
	■				Christ, whose glory fills the skies	6,7						
	■				From God Christ's deity came forth	443						
			■		Yo soy la luz del mundo / I am the world's true light					75		
					Matthew 17:1-9							
	■				Christ upon the mountain peak	129,130						
	■				I love to tell the story			64				
■					O light of Light, Love given birth	133,134						
		■		■	O wondrous type! O vision fair	136,137					■	■

Anthem	Solo	Handbells	Voicing		Collection	Composer
				Collect		
X				Create in Me		Johannes Brahms
X						Carl F Mueller
X				Hide Not Thou Thy Face	TUD	Richard Farrant
X				Lord, for Thy Tender Mercy's Sake	TUD	Richard Farrant
				Joel 2:1-2, 12-17		
X			SSSAATTTBB	Blow Up the Trumpet in Sion		Henry Purcell
X				Blow Ye the Trumpet in Zion		Francis Jackson
X				Fear Not, O Lord		William Harris
X				Return to the Lord, Your God		Carl Schalk
X			SAB	Sound Forth the Trumpet in Zion		Thomas Morley, ed Proulx
				Isaiah 58:1-12 (alt.)		
X			Unison	A Lenten Carol		Glen Darst
				Psalm 103:1-7, 8-14, 15-22		
X			SA	Bless the Lord My Soul, *Cantata 196*		J S Bach, arr Hopson
X				Bless the Lord, O My Soul		Austin Lovelace
X						Sam Batt Owens
X				Lord for Thy Tender Mercy's Sake	TUD	Richard Farrant
X				Not Only Unto Him, Bless..., *St. Paul*		Felix Mendelssohn
X				The Lord Has Established His Throne		Daniel Pinkham
X				The Paper Reeds..., *Peaceable Kingdom*		Randall Thompson
				2 Corinthians 5:20b-6:10		
X				The Beatitudes		Russian Chant
				Matthew 6:1-6, 16-21		
X				Ah, Thou Poor World	AFC 1	Johannes Brahms
X			TTBB	Lay Not Up for Yourselves		John Heath
X				Lay Up for Yourselves		Ned Rorem
X				Lord, Teach Us How to Pray Aright		Thomas Tallis
X				Steal Away		arr Dale Adelmann
X						arr William Dawson
X				Treasures in Heaven		Joseph W Clokey
	X			O Mortal World, *Cantata 95*	LIFT	J S Bach
	X			Steal Away		Spiritual, Various
				Psalm 51:1-17		
X				Asperges me, Domine		Multiple
X			Unison, 2 pt	Be Merciful, O Lord		John Karl Hirten
X				Create in Me, O God		Johannes Brahms
				Cast Me Not Away...		
				Grant Unto Me the Joy...		
X				Create in Me		Carl F Mueller
X				I'm Glad Salvation Is Free		Shelton Becton
X				Miserere mei, Deus		Multiple
X				Turn Thy Face from My Sins	OXCAB	Thomas Attwood
X					CON	Arthur Sullivan
X				Wash Me Throughly		G F Handel
X						Samuel Wesley
				Additional Music		
X			SATTB	Emendemus in melius		William Byrd
X				Give Rest O Christ *(may replace the Alleluias with Laudamus Domino)*		Russell Schulz-Widmar
X				Jesu, meine Freude	BFAS	J S Bach
X				My Spirit Longs for Thee	OXEA	John Dowland
X				Open Our Eyes		Leon Lumpkins
	X			Denn es gehe..., *Four Scriptural Songs*		Johannes Brahms
				Cantatas/Major Works		
X				199: Mein Herze schwimmt im Blut		J S Bach
X				Jesu, meine Freude, BWV 227 (motet)		J S Bach

Entrance	Sequence	Offertory	Communion	Postcommunion		H82	WLP	LEVAS II	VF	MHSO	CG descant	Inst descant
					Note: There is no Entrance Hymn on this day (see BCP, p. 264).							
	■				Almighty Lord Most High draw near [S]		888					
			■		Bless the Lord, my soul [P]		825					
		■			Bless the Lord, O my soul [P]			65				
					Come, ye disconsolate [S]			147				
	■			■	Eternal Lord of love, behold your Church [S]	149						
					O bless the Lord, my soul! [P]	411						
				■	The glory of these forty days [S]	143						
					Joel 2:1-2, 12-17							
	■				Before thy throne, O God, we kneel	574,575						■
■					Kind Maker of the world, O hear	152						
■					Lord Jesus, Sun of Righteousness	144						
					Isaiah 58:1-12							
		■			Creator of the earth and skies	148						
	■		■		Gracious Spirit, give your servants		782				▣	
			■		Lord, whose love through humble service	610						
■					Now quit your care	145						
■					O day of God, draw nigh	600,601						
					2 Corinthians 5:20b-6:10							
	■				Thou my everlasting portion			122				
		■			Lead us, heavenly Father, lead us	559						
					Matthew 6:1-6, 16-21							
	■				Give me a clean heart			124				
■					God himself is with us	475					■	
			■		In God we trust			55				
		■			I've decided to make Jesus my choice			68				
	■	■			Jesus, all my gladness	701						

Anthem	Solo	Handbells	Voicing		Collection	Composer
				Genesis 2:15-17; 3:1-7		
■				Adam Lay YBounden		Multiple
■				Provencal Carol		arr Donald Busarow
■				The Serpent	SEW	Thomas Pavlechko
■				The Truth from Above		arr Ralph Vaughan Williams
■				When Long Before Time		David Cherwien
				Psalm 32		
■				A Choral Flourish		Ralph Vaughan Williams
■			SAB	Be Glad You Righteous		Robert J Powell
■				Beati quorum via Ps. 119		Charles V Stanford
■			ATB	Blessed Is He Whose Unrighteousness...		Thomas Tomkins
■				Exultate Deo		Multiple
■				Exultate justi		Multiple
■			SST or SAB	Psalm 32		Paul Weber
■			TTBB	Whom the Lord Hath Forgiven		Alan MacMillan
				Romans 5:12-19		
■				Adam Lay YBounden		Multiple
■				Agnus Dei		Multiple
■				Behold the Lamb of God		J Brahms
■				Behold the Lamb of God, *Messiah*		G F Handel
■				God Remembers		Russell Schulz-Widmar
■				He That Shall Endure, *Elijah*		Felix Mendelssohn
■				Provencal Carol		arr Donald Busarow
■				Since By Man Came Death, *Messiah*		G F Handel
■				Since By Man Came Death	SEW	Thomas Pavlechko
■				The Truth From Above		arr Ralph Vaughan Williams
				Matthew 4:1-11		
■			Unison, 2 pt	Begone, Satan		Jan Bender
■				Jesus, So Lowly		Harold Friedell
■				Jesus Walked That Lonesome Valley		arr John Ferguson
■						arr William Dawson
■				The Serpent		Thomas Pavlechko
■				The Temptation of Christ		Lloyd Pfautsch
	■			Ein feste Burg ist unser Gott, *Cantata 80*		J S Bach
	■			I Ain't Got Weary Yet	SOS	Spiritual, arr Boatner
				Jesus Walked That Lonesome Valley		Various
				Additional Music		
■			SATB, str	Sweet Spirit, Comfort Me		Russell Schulz-Widmar
				Cantatas/Major Works		
				40: Dazu ist erschienen der Sohn Gottes		J S Bach

Entrance	Sequence	Offertory	Communion	Postcommunion		H82	WLP	LEVAS II	VF	MHSO	CG descant	Inst descant
					Genesis 2:15-17; 3:1-7							
	▨				Creator of the earth and skies	148						
	▨				Wilt thou forgive that sin, where I begun	140,141						
					Romans 5:12-19							
	▨				Praise to the Holiest in the height	445,446					▨	
					Matthew 4:1-11							
				▨	Forty days and forty nights (1)					84		
▨	▨				Forty days and forty nights	150						
				▨	From God Christ's deity came forth	443						
				▨	It is well with my soul			188				
		▨	▨		Lord, who throughout these forty days	142						▨
		▨	▨		Now let us all with one accord	146,147						
		▨	▨		O love, how deep, how broad, how high	448,449					▨	▨
			▨		Sweet hour of prayer			178				
▨				▨	The glory of these forty days	143						

Anthem	Solo	Handbells	Voicing		Collection	Composer
				Genesis 12:1-4a		
■			SSA	God's Promise		Samuel Adler
■				Magnificat		Multiple
■				Offertory, *Requiem Mass*		Multiple
				Psalm 121		
	■		Unison	A Song of Trust		Charles V Stanford
■				Auxilium meum		Pierre Passereau
■			2 pt	Coverdale's Psalm 121		John Bertalot
■				He Watching over Israel, *Elijah*		Felix Mendelssohn
■				I Lift My Eyes to the Hills		Jean Berger
■			2 pt treble			Paul Bouman
■			Mixed canon			David Hurd
■						John Rutter
■						Leo Sowerby
■			SSA	Lift Thine Eyes, *Elijah*		Felix Mendelssohn
■			TTBB	Psalm 121		Samuel Adler
■			SSA			Charles Callahan
■						Zoltan Kodaly
■			2 pt			Robert J Powell
■				Psalm CXXI, *Cantata 71*		J S Bach
■				Total Praise		Richard Smallwood
	■	■		I Will Lift Up Mine Eyes	LIFT	Peter Pindar Stearns
■				Psalm 121		Harold Friedell
				Romans 4:1-5, 13-17		
■				Magnificat		Multiple
■				Offertory, *Requiem Mass*		Multiple
■				Salvation Unto Us Has Come	BFAS	J S Bach
				John 3:1-17		
■				Also hat Gott die Welt geliebet		Gallus Dressler
■				As Moses Lifted Up the Serpent		Edward Bairstow
■				Blessed Assurance		Nancy Wertsch
■			2 pt	God Sent His Son into the World		G F Handel
■				God So Loved the World		Jan Bender
■						Bob Chilcott
■						Katherine K Davis
■						Hugo Distler
■						Orlando Gibbons
■						John Goss
■			Unison or 2 pt			John Horman
■			SA			Joel Martinson,
■			SSATBB			Michael Praetorius
■						Heinrich Schütz
■						John Stainer
■			SAB, inst			G P Telemann
■						Melchoir Vulpius
■						David Ashley White
■				Offertory, *Requiem Mass*		Multiple
■				Sicut Moses serpentem		Heinrich Schütz
		■		Also hat Gott die Welt geliebt, *Cantata 68*		J. S. Bach
		■		Behold the Son of God	LIFT	W A Mozart
				Additional Music		
■				In Thee, O Lord, Have I Trusted	CON	G F Handel
■				Lord, Thee I Love with All My Heart	BFAS	J S Bach
				Cantatas/Major Works		
				173: Erhöhtes Fleisch und Blut		J S Bach

Entrance	Sequence	Offertory	Communion	Postcommunion		H82	WLP	LEVAS II	VF	MHSO	CG descant	Inst descant
				■	I to the hills will lift mine eyes [P]	668						
					Genesis 12:1-4a							
	■				Now let us all with one accord	146,147						
		■			Praise our great and gracious Lord	393						
■					The God of Abraham praise	401					■	
					Romans 4:1-5, 13-17							
	■	■			God it was who said to Abraham(1,5)					85		
	■			■	How firm a foundation, ye saints of the Lord	636,637						■
	■				I call on thee, Lord Jesus Christ	634						
		■		■	We've come this far by faith			208				
					John 3:1-17							
				■	And now, O Father, mindful of the love	337						
		■			Lift high the cross	473						■
	■				O love, how deep, how broad, how high	448,449					■	
			■		The great Creator of the worlds	489						
				■	When Christ was lifted from the earth	603,604						

Anthem	Solo	Handbells	Voicing		Collection	Composer
				Exodus 17:1-7		
				A Welcome Song – A Song for Baptism	SEW	Thomas Pavlechko
				As Panting Deer Desire the Waterbrooks		David Ashley White
				Like As the Hart		Herbert Howells
				Sicut Cervus		Multiple
				The Lord is a Mighty God		Felix Mendelssohn
				Jesus Is a Rock in a Weary Land		Spiritual, Various
				Psalm 95		
				Come, Let Us Rejoice		John Amner
				Come, Let Us Sing to the Lord		Carl MaultsBy
				O Come Let Us Sing Unto the Lord		Jean Berger
			TTBB			Emma Lou Diemer
						Anthony Piccolo
						K Lee Scott
				O Come Let Us Worship		G P Palestrina
			SSAATTBB	O Come Let Us Worship, *All Night Vigil*		Sergei Rachmaninoff
			2 pt	Rejoice Be Glad in the Lord		Robert Leaf
			SSATB	Venite, exultemus Domino		J P Sweelinck
				O Come, Let Us Worship	LIFT	G F Handel
				Romans 5:1-11		
				Agnus Dei		Multiple
				All Who Believe and Are Baptized	BFAS	J S Bach
				Also hat Gott die Welt geliebet		Gallus Dressler
				And With His Stripes, *Messiah*		G F Handel
				Behold the Lamb of God		J Brahms
				Behold the Lamb of God, *Messiah*		G F Handel
				God Remembers		Russell Schulz-Widmar
			2 pt	God Sent His Son Into the World		G F Handel
				God So Loved the World		Multiple (see Lent 2A)
				He That Shall Endure to the End, *Elijah*		Felix Mendelssohn
				Salvation Unto Us Has Come		J S Bach
				Since By Man Came Death, *Messiah*		G F Handel
				Since By Man Came Death	SEW	Thomas Pavlechko
				Surely He Hath Borne…, *Messiah*		G F Handel
				Surely He Hath Borne Our Griefs		Carl Heinrich Graun
						Hugo Distler
				The Truth From Above		arr Ralph V Williams
			3 pt	Vere languores		André Campra
			3 pt or SATB			Antonio Lotti
						Tomás Luis de Victoria
				Wondrous Love		Various
				John 4:5-42		
				A Welcome Song – A Song for Baptism	SEW	Thomas Pavlechko
				As Panting Deer Desire the Waterbrooks		David Ashley White
				Come, to the Water		John Foley
				Eternal Life		Walter Hawkins
				God Is a Spirit		W Sterndale Bennett
						Alexander Kopylov
						Randall Thompson
				Like As the Hart		Herbert Howells
				Sicut cervus		Multiple
			SA	Sir, Come Down Before My Child Dies		Jan Bender
				Thee We Adore		T Frederick Candlyn
				I Just Came from the Fountain	SOS	Spiritual, arr Boatner
				Additional Music		
				Surely It Is God Who Saves Me		Jack Noble White
				Cantatas/ Major Works		
				13: Meine Seufzer, meine Tränen		J S Bach

						H82	WLP	LEVAS II	VF	MHSO	CG descant	Inst descant
		▓			To God with gladness sing [P]	399						
					Exodus 17:1-7							
▓		▓			Come, thou fount of every blessing	686		111			▓	
▓					Glorious things of thee are spoken	522,523						
			▓		Guide me, O thou great Jehovah	690						
		▓			O Food to pilgrims given	308,309						
					O God, unseen yet ever near	332						
▓					Rock of ages, cleft for me	685						▓
			▓		Shepherd of souls, refresh and flesh	343					▓	
▓		▓			Surely it is God who saves me	678,679						
					Romans 5:1-11							
▓					Camina, pueblo de Dios/Walk on, O people of God		739					
		▓			Hail, thou once despised Jesus	495						▓
▓					O Love of God, how strong and true	455,456					▓	
			▓		There is a balm in Gilead (1-2)	676		203				
		▓			You, Lord, we praise in songs of celebration	319						
					John 4:5-42							
			▓		As longs the deer for cooling streams	658						
					As panting deer desire the waterbrooks		727					
					Draw nigh and take the Body of the Lord	327,328						
					I heard the voice of Jesus say	692						
					In your mercy, Lord, you called me	706						
					Jesus, Lover of my soul	699		79			▓	
					Lord, my soul is thirsting			166		148		
					O Jesus, joy of loving hearts	649,650						
					O love that casts out fear	700						
		▓			The first one ever, oh, ever to know	673						
			▓		When, like the woman at the well				24			

Anthem	Solo	Handbells	Voicing		Collection	Composer
				I Samuel 16:1-13		
	■			Little David, Play on Your Harp		Spiritual, Various
				Psalm 23		
■				Psalm 23		Multiple
■				My Shepherd Is Lord		Harrison Oxley
■				The Lord Is My Shepherd		Howard Goodall
■				The Lord My Shepherd		David Ashley White
■			2 pt canon			Gregg Smith
	■			Psalm 23		Multiple
■				The Lord Is My Shepherd	LIFT	Peter Pindar Stearns
				Ephesians 5:8-14		
■				King Jesus Hath A Garden	100 CFC	harm Charles Wood
■			Unison	Now Are Ye Light in the Lord		Healey Willan
■				Sleepers, Wake!	AFC 1	Felix Mendelssohn
■			Unison or SATB	Wachet auf		J S Bach
■				Ye Were Sometimes Darkness		Randall Thompson
	■		Bass	The People That Walked..., *Messiah*		G F Handel
				John 9:1-41		
■				Amazing Grace		arr David Ashley White
■				Give God the Glory		James Hill
■			Unison	My Eyes for Beauty Pine	OXEA	Herbert Howells
■				Open Our Eyes		Will C MacFarlane
■						Leon Lumpkins
■				The Blind Man		arr William Grant Still
■				The Pool of Bethesda		Leo Sowerby
				Additional Music		
■				There Is a Balm		arr William Dawson
	■			I Know the Lord Laid His Hands on Me		Spiritual, Various
	■			There Is a Balm		Spiritual, Various

Entrance	Sequence	Offertory	Communion	Postcommunion		H82	WLP	LEVAS II	VF	MHSO	CG descant	Inst descant
			X		My Shepherd will supply my need [P]	664						
					The King of love my shepherd is [P]	645,646					X	
					The Lord is my shepherd [P]			104				
					The Lord my God my shepherd is [P]	663						
					1 Samuel 16:1-13							
X					God moves in a mysterious way	677						
	X				In the bulb there is a flower					86		
X					Seek the Lord while he wills to be found	S 217ff						
					Ephesians 5:8-14							
X					Awake, O sleeper, rise from death	547						
		X			God to enfold you					146		
X	X	X			I want to walk as a child of the light	490						X
	X				Longing for light, we wait in darkness					59		
X					Lord Jesus, Sun of Righteousness	144						
X					O splendor of God's glory bright	5						
			X		So the day dawn for me		750					
X	X				When from bondage we are summoned		753,754				X	
					John 9:1-41							
X					Christ, whose glory fills the skies	6,7						
			X		Deck thyself, my soul, with gladness	339						
X	X				Eternal light, shine in my heart	465,466						
		X			God, creator, source of healing				93		0	
			X		God of mercy, God of grace	538						
					How wondrous and great thy works, God of praise!	532,533					X	
		X			I'll praise my Maker while I've breath	429						
			X		I heard the voice of Jesus say	692						
				X	Lord God, you now have set your servant free	499						
					Lord, you have fulfilled your word		891					
X	X				O for a thousand tongues to sing	493						X
			X		The light of Christ					80		
			X		The Lord is my light			58				

	Voicing	Title	Collection	Composer
		Ezekiel 37:1-14		
		Dry Bones		Spiritual, Various
		Dry Bones		Mark Hayes
		Dem Dry Bones		Hall Johnson
		Psalm 130		
		De profundis		Multiple
		Hear My Cry, Holy One		David Ashley White
		Out of the Depths		Multiple
	SAB			John Horman
	SATB, SAB			W A Mozart
	2 pt			K Lee Scott
				Heinrich Schütz
		Out of the Deep, *Requiem*		John Rutter
	SAB	Out of the Deep		Henry Purcell
	ATB			Thomas Tompkins
		Psalm 130		Multiple
	SAATB	Lord, to Thee I Make My Moan		Thomas Weelkes
	TTB	Si iniquitates observaveris		Samuel Wesley
		Aus tiefer Not schrei..., *Cantata 38*		J S Bach
	(trio)	Aus der Tiefen rufe ich..., *Cantata 131*		J S Bach
		Romans 8:6-11		
		In Paradisum, *Requiem*		Multiple
		Verily, Verily I Say Unto You	AFC 1	Thomas Tallis
		Jesu meine Freude, BWV 227, (motet)		J S Bach
		John 11:1-45		
		Agnus Dei, *Requiem*		John Rutter
		I Am the Resurrection		Jan Bender
				John Carter
				Gallus Dressler
				Thomas Morely
		I Am the Resurrection and the Life	CHAN	Gallus Dressler
	SATB/SATB			Heinrich Schütz
	SA			Healey Willan
				David H Williams
		In Paradisum, *Requiem*		Multiple
		Jesus, So Lowly		Harold Friedell
		Lord, Let Your Own Sweet Angels	E-Libris	J S Bach
		Lord, Thee I Love with All My Heart	BFAS	J S Bach
		Verily, Verily I Say Unto You	AFC 1	Thomas Tallis
		Additional Music		
		Come My Way, My Truth, My Life		Harold Friedell
	Baritone	The Call, *Five Mystical Songs*		Ralph Vaughan Williams

Entrance	Sequence	Offertory	Communion	Postcommunion		H82	WLP	LEVAS II	VF	MHSO	CG descant	Inst descant
			■		From deepest woe I cry to thee [P]	151						
					Out of the depths I call [P]	666						
					Ezekiel 37:1-14							
■		■			Breath of God, life-bearing wind				59		O	
			■		Breathe on me, Breath of God	508						
				■	Go forth for God; go to the world in peace	347						
			■		Let it breathe on me			116				
■					Put forth, O God, thy Spirit's might	521						
			■		Spirit of the living God			115				
					Romans 8:6-11							
	■				Come down, O Love divine	516					■	
	■				Come, Gracious Spirit, heavenly Dove	512					■	
	■				Come, Holy Ghost, Creator blest			112			■	
	■				Come, Holy Spirit, heavenly Dove	510					■	
	■				Filled with the Spirit's power		741				■	
	■				Holy Spirit, ever living	511					O	
	■				O splendor of God's glory bright	5						
	■				Spirit divine, attend our prayers	509						
	■				Spirit of God, descend upon my heart			119				
					John 11:1-45							
			■		Awake, O sleeper, rise from death	547						
			■		Eternal light, shine in my heart	465,466						
			■		I am the bread of life (4,5)	335						■
			■		In deepest night, in darkest days				97			
			■		In the bulb there is a flower					86		
				■	Lord, whose love through humble service	610						
			■		O bless the Lord, my soul	411						
■			■		O for a thousand tongues to sing	493					■	
			■		O Love of God, how strong and true	455,456					■	
			■		Take my hand, precious Lord			106				
■			■		Thine arm, O Lord, in days of old	567					■	
			■		Thou art the Way, to thee alone	457						
			■		When Jesus wept	715						

Anthem	Solo	Handbells	Voicing		Collection	Composer
				LITURGY OF THE PALMS Matthew 21:1-11		
			Unison	A Sacred Song for P Sun/ Hosanna to...		Richard DeLong
				Benedictus qui venit		Multiple
				Hosanno filio David		Tomas Luis de Victoria
				Lift Up Your Heads	16th	John Amner
						William Mathias
				Lift Up Your Heads, *Messiah*		G F Handel
				Pueri Hebraeorum		Multiple
				Ride On, King Jesus		Robert Shaw/Alice Parker
				Ride On! Ride On in Majesty!		T Frederick Candlyn
			SATB, Vla	Who Is This		John Ferguson
				Ride On, King Jesus		Hall Johnson, et al
				Psalm 118:1-2, 19-29		
			Sop/Unis treble	Benedictus qui venit, *Messe Basse*		Gabriel Faure
				Lift Up Your Heads	16th	John Amner
						William Mathias
				Lift Up Your Heads, *Messiah*		G F Handel
				LITURGY OF THE WORD Isaiah 50:4-9a		
				And with His Stripes, *Messiah*		G F Handel
				Psalm 31:9-16		
				In te, Domine		Josquin des Prez, H Schütz
			SATTB	In te speravi		G P Palestrina
				In Thee, O Lord, Have I Trusted	CON	G F Handel
				Philippians 2:5-11		
				Adoramus te, Christe		Multiple
				At the Name of Jesus		Ralph Vaughan Williams
				Christus factus est		Multiple
				Jesu, dulcis memoria		Multiple
			SAB	Jesus, Name of Wondrous Love		Everett Titcomb
				Let This Mind Be in You		Lee Hoiby
			SSA or SAB	Non nobis, Domine		(attr.) William Byrd *(et al)*
				Praise to You Lord Jesus	CHAN	Heinrich Schütz
				Matthew 26:14-27:66 or Matthew 27:11-54		
				A Lamb Goes Uncomplaining Forth	CHAN	Hugo Distler
				How Hast Thou Offended		Heinrich Schütz
				In monte Oliveti		Multiple
			2 pt	Into Jerusalem Jesus Rode		Alfred V. Fedak
				Tristis est anima mea		Multiple
				Chorales from The Passions: Matthew/John		J S Bach
				Additional Music		
			3-pt treble	Agnus Dei, *Messe Basse*		Gabriel Faure *(et al)*
				Craftsman's Carol		Thomas Pavlechko
				Crux fidelis		Multiple
				Faithful Cross		Thomas Pavlechko
				Jesus, So Lowly		Harold Friedell
				Lamb of God		Multiple
				Pange Lingua/Sing, My Tongue		Multiple
				Solus ad Victimam/Alone to Sacrifice	AFC 1	Kenneth Leighton
				The Crown of Roses	100 Carols	Tchaikovsky
				The Lamb		John Tavener
			Unison	The Royal Banners of Our King		Russell Schulz-Widmar
				The Way to Jerusalem		Harold Friedell
				Were You There		arr Harold Friedell
				Cantatas/Major Works		
				182: Himmelskönig, sei willkommen		J S Bach
				St. Matthew Passion		Schütz, Bach, *(et al)*
				Stabat Mater		Multiple

						H82	WLP	LEVAS II	VF	MHSO	CG descant	Inst descant
					At the Liturgy of the Palms: Matthew 21:1-11							
▨					Palm Sunday Anthems	153						
▨					All glory, laud, and honor	154,155						▨
▨					Mantos y palmas esparciendo / Filled with excitement		728					
▨					Ride on, King Jesus			97				
▨					Ride on, ride on in majesty	156						
▨					Sanna, sannanina					91		
					Isaiah 50:4-9a							
	▨			▨	Alone thou goest forth, O Lord	164						
	▨				Hail, thou once despised Jesus! (1-2)	495						▨
	▨				To mock your reign, O dearest Lord	170						
					Philippians 2:5-11							
	▨				Cross of Jesus, cross of sorrow	160						
	▨				Morning glory, starlit sky (4-6)	585					▨	
	▨				The flaming banners of our king	161						
	▨				The royal banners forward go	162						
	▨				What wondrous love is this	439						▨
					Matthew (26:14-27:10) 27:11-54							
		▨			Ah, holy Jesus, how hast thou offended	158						
		▨			And now, O Father, mindful of the love (1-2)	337						
		▨			Let thy blood in mercy poured	313						
		▨			My song is love unknown	458						
		▨			Nature with open volume stands	434						
		▨			O Jesus, scourged, derided, mocked			49				▨
		▨			O sacred head, sore wounded	168,169	735	36				
		▨		▨	When I survey the wondrous cross	474					▨	
				▨	Would you share Christ's passion?				42			

Anthem	Solo	Handbells	Voicing			Collection	Composer
				Isaiah 42:1-9			
	▪			Ein jeder läuft, der in den Schranken			G P Telemann
				Psalm 36:5-11			
▪				How Precious Is Thy Loving Kindness			Samuel Adler
▪							Daniel Pinkham
▪			TB	Thy Mercy Jehovah			Benedetto Marcello
▪				Thy Mercy O Lord Reacheth Unto...			Paul C Edwards
▪	▪		SS	Loving Kindness			Henry Purcell
				Hebrews 9:11-15			
▪			Unison	The Promise of Eternal Inheritance			Rudolf Moser
				John 12:1-11			
▪				A Litany/Drop, Drop, Slow Tears		AFC 4	William Walton
▪				Jesu, meine Freude		BFAS	J S Bach
▪			SATB, inst	The Anointing, *Sacred Symphonies*			Alice Parker
	▪		Soprano	How Beautiful Are the Feet, *Messiah*			G F Handel

Entrance	Sequence	Offertory	Communion	Postcommunion		H82	WLP	LEVAS II	VF	MHSO	CG descant	Inst descant
				■	We sing the praise of him who died [S]	471						
					Isaiah 42:1-9							
		■			Ancient of Days, who sittest throned in glory	363						
■		■		■	Jesus shall reign where'er the sun	544					■	
		■			Thy strong word did cleave the darkness	381						■
■					Weary of all trumpeting	572						
					Hebrews 9:11-15							
■		■			Come, thou fount of every blessing	686	111				■	
		■			Cross of Jesus, cross of sorrow	160						
			■		Draw nigh and take the Body of the Lord	327,328						
■					Glory be to Jesus	479						
	■				Holy Father, great Creator	368						■
			■		Let thy Blood in mercy poured	313						
					John 12:1-11							
	■				God himself is with us	475					■	
			■		Holy woman, graceful giver				1			
					Jesus, all my gladness	701						
					Jesus, the very thought of thee	642						
					Just as I am, without one plea	693	137		82,83, 84			■
					There's a wideness in God's mercy	469,470						

Anthem	Solo	Handbells	Voicing		Collection	Composer
				Isaiah 49:1-7		
	■			Hear Ye, Israel, *Elijah*		Felix Mendelssohn
	■			Sing O Heavens		Emma Lou Diemer
				Psalm 71:1-14		
■				Go Not Far From Me O God		Nicola Zingarelli
■			SSATB	Herr, auf dich Traus ich		Heinrich Schütz
■				In Thee, O Lord		Jane Marshall
■			2 pt	O Lord, My God..., Bist Du bei mir		J S Bach, arr Hopson
				1 Corinthians 1:18-31		
■				Crux fidelis		Multiple
■				Faithful Cross		Thomas Pavlechko
■				The Foolishness Carol		Austin Lovelace
■				The Wisdom of God		Austin Lovelace
				John 12:20-36		
■				As Moses Lifted Up the Serpent		Edward Bairstow
■				Jesus, So Lowly		Harold Friedell
■				Lift Up Your Heads	16th	John Amner
■				Lift Up Your Heads, *Messiah*		G F Handel
■				Sicut Moses serpentem		Heinrich Schütz
■				The Way to Jerusalem		Harold Friedell
■			SATB, vla	Who Is This?		John Ferguson
■			SSATB	Yet a Little While		Knut Nystedt

						H82	WLP	LEVAS II	VF	MHSO	CG descant	Inst descant
				■	My song is love unknown (1-2,7) [S]	458						
					Isaiah 49:1-7							
■					Christ, whose glory fills the skies	6,7						
	■				God of mercy, God of grace	538						
■					How wondrous and great thy works, God of praise!	532,533						■
					1 Corinthians 1:18-31							
			■		Beneath the cross of Jesus	498						
	■				Cross of Jesus, cross of sorrow	160						
		■			In the cross of Christ I glory	441,442						
			■		Jesus, keep me near the cross			29				
■					Nature with open volume stands	434						
			■		On a hill far away stood an old rugged cross			38				
■					We sing the praise of him who died	471						
		■			When I survey the wondrous cross	474					■	
					John 12:20-36							
	■				I heard the voice of Jesus say	692						
	■				I want to walk as a child of the Light	490						■
			■		O Jesus, I have promised	655					■	
		■			The great Creator of the worlds	489						
	■				When Christ was lifted from the earth	603,604						

Anthem	Solo	Handbells	Voicing		Collection	Composer
				Isaiah 50:4-9a		
	■		Alto	He Was Despised, *Messiah*		G F Handel
				How Hast Thou Offended		Heinrich Schütz
				Psalm 70		
■				Deus in adjutorium		J Pachelbel
■				Eile, mich, Gott, zu erretten		Heinrich Schütz
■				Haste Thee, O God	AFC 1	Adrian Batten
■				Make Haste		Alan Hovhaness
			TTBB	Psalm 70		Leo Sowerby
				Hebrews 12:1-3		
■				Adoramus te		Multiple
■				Christus factus est		Multiple
■				He Endured the Cross		Carl H Graun
■				Seeing We Also		Leo Sowerby
				John 13:21-32		
	■			Adoramus te		Multiple
■				Ah, Holy Jesus	AFC 4	arr Roger T Petrich
■				Christus factus est		Multiple

Entrance	Sequence	Offertory	Communion	Postcommunion		H82	WLP	LEVAS II	VF	MHSO	CG descant	Inst descant
					Isaiah 50:4-9a							
				▓	Alone thou goest forth, O Lord	164						
			▓		Bread of heaven, on thee we feed	323						
			▓		Let thy Blood in mercy poured	313						
▓					To mock your reign, O dearest Lord	170						
					Hebrews 12:1-3							
▓					Hail, thou once despised Jesus	495						▓
	▓				Lo! what a cloud of witnesses	545						
▓					The head that once was crowned with thorns	483						
					John 13:21-32							
	▓				Ah, holy Jesus, how hast thou offended	158						
			▓		Bread of the world, in mercy broken	301						
▓		▓		▓	O love, how deep, how broad, how high	448,449					▓	

Anthem	Solo	Handbells	Voicing		Collection	Composer
				Exodus 12:1-4 [5-10] 11-14		
				Psalm 116:1-2, 12-19		
■				What Shall I Render to My God		Austin Lovelace
				1 Corinthians 11:23-26		
■				Ave verum		Multiple
■				Of the Glorious Body Telling		Multiple
■				Pange lingua		Multiple
■				Tantum ergo/Genitori, Genitoque		Multiple
■				Verily, Verily I Say Unto You	AFC 1	Thomas Tallis
■				Words of Institution	SEW Vol. 11	Thomas Pavlechko
				John 13:1-17, 31b-35		
■				A Litany/Drop, Drop, Slow Tears	AFC 4	William Walton
■				Asperges me, Domine		Multiple
■				Christus factus est		Multiple
■			SAB	Non nobis, Domine		attr. William Byrd, *(et al)*
■				Ubi caritas		Maurice Duruflé
	■			Behold the Son of God	LIFT	W A Mozart
				Additional Music		
■				Beautiful Savior		F Melius Christiansen
■				Jesu, dulcis memoria		Multiple
■				O Sacrum Convivium *ed. w/out alleluias*		Multiple
■				O Salutaris Hostia		Multiple
■				Thee We Adore		T Frederick Candlyn
				Cantatas/Major Works		
				180: Schmücke dich, o liebe Seele		J S Bach

Entrance	Sequence	Offertory	Communion	Postcommunion		H82	WLP	LEVAS II	VF	MHSO	CG descant	Inst descant
				■	Go to dark Gethsemane [S]	171						
					Exodus 12:1-4, (5-10) 11-14							
■		■			What wondrous love is this, O my soul!	439						■
					1 Corinthians 11:23-26							
					As we proclaim your death				80			
					Do this in remembrance of me			272				
					In remembrance of me, eat this bread			149				
					Let us break bread together on our knees	325		152				
					Now, my tongue, the mystery telling	329, 330, 331						
					Pan de Vida, cuerpo del Señor					93		
					This is my body given for you			155				
■					When Jesus died to save us	322						
					Zion, praise thy Savior, singing	320						
					John 13:1-17,31b-35							
					A new commandment that I give to you					92		
					As in that upper room you left your seat		729,730					
					Three holy days enfold us now		731, 732, 733					
					Thou, who at thy first Eucharist didst pray	315						
					You laid aside your rightful reputation		734					
					At the footwashing:							
					Brother, sister, let me serve you					124	94	
					God is love, and where true love is	576,577						
					Jesu, Jesu, fill us with your love	602		74				
					Ubi caritas et amor		831					
					Where charity and love prevail	581						
					Where true charity and love dwell	606						
					At the stripping of the altar:							
					Stay with me		826					

Anthem	Solo	Handbells	Voicing		Collection	Composer
				Isaiah 52:13-53:12		
■				Agnus Dei		Multiple
■				And with His Stripes, *Messiah*		G F Handel
■				Behold the Lamb of God, *Messiah*		G F Handel
■				Furwahr! Er trug..., Surely He Hath		Carl Heinrich Graun
■				God So Loved the World		Jan Bender
■						Bob Chilcott
■						Katherine K Davis
■						Hugo Distler
■						Orlando Gibbons
■						John Goss
■			Unison or 2 pt			John Horman
■			SA			Joel Martinson
■			SSATBB			Michael Praetorius
■						Heinrich Schütz
■						John Stainer
■			SAB, inst			G P Telemann
■						Melchoir Vulpius
■						David Ashley White
■				Surely He Hath Borne Our Griefs, *Messiah*		G F Handel
■						Carl Heinrich Graun
■						Hugo Distler
■			3 pt	Vere languores		André Campra
■			3 pt or SATB			Antonio Lotti
■						Tomás Luis de Victoria
	■			Messiah, Part 2		G F Handel
				Psalm 22		
■				He Trusted in God, *Messiah*		G F Handel
■				O vos omnes		Multiple
■				When We Are Tempted to Deny...		Sally Ann Morris
■				He Was Despised, *Messiah*		G F Handel
				Hebrews 10:16-25		
■				Agnus Dei		Multiple
■				Ave Verum		Multiple
■				Christus factus est		Multiple
				Hebrews 4:14-16; 5:7-9 (alt.)		
■				Adoramus te		Multiple
■				Christus factus est		Multiple
				John 18:1-19:42		
■				Chorales, *St. John Passion*	E-Libris	J S Bach
■				Crucifixus		Hall Johnson
■				Crucifixus, *St. John Passion*		J S Bach
■				How Hast Thou Offended		Heinrich Schütz
■				In monte Oliveti		Multiple
■				Nolo mortem peccatoris	16th	Thomas Morley
■				Stabat Mater		Multiple
■				Tenebrae factae sunt		Multiple
■				Tristis est anima mea		Multiple
				Additional Music		
■				Adoramus te Christe		Multiple
■				Crux fidelis		Multiple
■				Faithful Cross/Cross of Glory		Thomas Pavlechko
■				Improperium	CHE	Orlando Lassus
■				Were You There		arr Harold Friedell
				Cantatas/Major Works		
				Stabat Mater		Multiple
				The Passion According to St. John		J S Bach, et al

						H82	WLP	LEVAS II	VF	MHSO	CG descant	Inst descant
					Note: *There is no Entrance Hymn on this day (see BCP, p. 276).*							
	×				For this day, hymns in this column are for singing after the sermon;							
		×			hymns in this column are for singing before the cross;							
			×		and hymns in this column are for singing to end the service after the Solemn Collects.							
					Isaiah 52:13-53:12							
					Ah, holy Jesus, how hast thou offended	158						
					O sacred head, sore wounded	168,169	735	36				▨
					To mock your reign, O dearest Lord	170						
					Hebrews 10:16-25							
					Alone thou goest forth, O Lord	164						
					Cross of Jesus, cross of sorrow	160						
					Hebrews 4:14-16; 5:7-9							
					From God Christ's deity came forth	443						
					There is a green hill far away	167			49			
					John 18:1-19:42							
					At the cross her vigil keeping	159						
					Every time I think about Jesus [Calvary]			32				
					Faithful cross, above all other		737					
					Go to dark Gethsemane	171						
					In the cross of Christ I glory	441,442						
					Jesus, keep me near the cross			29				
					King of my life I crown thee now			31				
					Lord Christ, when first thou cam'st to earth	598					▨	
					Morning glory, starlit sky	585					▨	
					O how he loves you and me			35				
					On a hill far away stood an old rugged cross			38				
					Sing, my tongue the glorious battle	165,166						
					Sunset to sunrise changes now	163						
					There is a fountain filled with blood			39				
					They crucified my Lord			33				
					Were you there when they crucified my Lord?	172		37(1-3)				▨
					When I survey the wondrous cross	474					▨	
					When Jesus came to Golgotha		736					
					When on the cross of Calvary			34				
					Would you share Christ's passion?				42			

Anthem	Solo	Handbells	Voicing		Collection	Composer
				Job 14:1-14		
■				The Paper Reeds..., *Peaceable Kingdom*		Randall Thompson
				Lamentations 3:1-9, 19-24 (alt)		
■				De profundis		Multiple
■				Hear My Cry, Holy One		David Ashley White
■				Out of the Depths		Multiple
■			SAB			John Horman
■			SATB or SAB			W A Mozart
■			2 pt			K Lee Scott
■						Heinrich Schütz
■				Out of the Deep, *Requiem*		John Rutter
■			SAB	Out of the Deep		Henry Purcell
■			ATB			Thomas Tompkins
■				Psalm 130		Multiple
■			SAATB	Lord, to Thee I Make My Moan		Thomas Weelkes
■			TTB	Si iniquitates observaveris		Samuel Wesley
■	■			Aus tiefer Not schrei ..., *Cantata 38*		J S Bach
■				Aus der Tiefen rufe ich..., *Cantata 131*		J S Bach
				Psalm 31:1-4, 15-16		
■				In te, Domine		Heinrich Schütz
■			SAB	In te, Domine speravi		D Buxtehude
■			Unison	In Thee, O Lord Do I Put My Trust		Jan Bender
■				In Thee, O Lord, Have I Trusted	CON	G F Handel
				1 Peter 4:1-8		
■			SSA or SSAA	If Ye Love Me		Harvey B Gaul
■			SSA			Daniel Pinkham
■						Thomas Tallis
■			SSA			Healey Willan
■						Philip Wilby
				Matthew 27:57-66		
■				Sepulto Domino		Tomás Luis de Victoria
				John 19:38-42 (alt)		
■				Sepulto Domino		Tomás Luis de Victoria
				Additional Music		
■				Ave Verum		Multiple
				Cantatas/Major Works		
				38: Aus tiefer Not schrei ich zu dir		J S Bach

						H82	WLP	LEVAS II	VF	MHSO	CG descant	Inst descant
					Note: There is no Entrance Hymn on this day (see BCP, p. 283).							
					Job 14:1-14							
					From deepest woe I cry to thee	151						
					Immortal, invisible, God only wise	423						▨
					Out of the depths I call	666						
					Lamentations 3:1-9,19-24							
					The steadfast love of the Lord never ceases		755					
					1 Peter 4:1-8							
					In deepest night, in darkest days				97			
					O love, how deep, how broad, how high (1-4,6)	448,449					▨	
					O Love of God, how strong and true (1-3)	455,456					▨	
					Matthew 27:57-66							
					King of my life I crown thee now			31				
					My song is love unknown (1-2,6-7)	458						
					O sorrow deep!	173						
					Were you there when they crucified my Lord?	172		37(1-3)				▨
					John 19:38-42							
					My song is love unknown (1-2,6-7)	458						
					O sorrow deep!	173						
					Were you there when they crucified my Lord?	172		37(1-3)				

Anthem	Solo	Handbells	Voicing		Collection	Composer
				Zephaniah 3:14-20		
▪			Unison	Sing Aloud, O Daughter of Zion		John Eggert
▪	▪		SAB, Sop solo	Sing, O Daughters of Zion		Jan Bender
	▪			Rejoice Greatly, *Messiah*		G F Handel
				Psalm 98		
▪				Cantate Domino		Multiple
▪				Sing to the Lord a New Song		Multiple
				Romans 6:3-11		
▪			SSAB	Alleluia, Christ Our Passover		Jan Bender
				Canticle for Communion		Jane Marshall
				Christ, Our Passover		Alan Gibbs
						John Goss
▪			SATB, Brass			Richard Dirksen
						Will C MacFarlane
		▪	2 pt			Robert J Powell
				Christ the Lord Is Risen Again		Richard Proulx
				Easter Triumph		Ronald Arnatt
				Since by Man Came Death, *Messiah*		G F Handel
				Since by Man Came Death	SEW MMVI	Thomas Pavlechko
				Psalm 114		
▪				Psalm 114		Zoltan Kodaly
▪				When Israel Came Out...,(In exita Israel)		William Byrd
						Hans Leo Hassler
						Samuel Wesley
				Matthew 28:1-10		
▪				Blessed Art Thou..., *All Night Vigil*		Sergei Rachmaninoff
▪				Today Hath Salvation..., *All Night Vigil*		Sergei Rachmaninoff
▪				When Thou, O Lord..., *All Night Vigil*		Sergei Rachmaninoff
▪				We Have Seen Thy..., *All Night Vigil*		Sergei Rachmaninoff
				See also Easter Day		

						H82	WLP	LEVAS II	VF	MHSO	CG descant	Inst descant
					It is preferable to sing the appointed Psalm or Canticle after each lesson,							
			·		*but the following suitable hymns and songs may be sung instead.*							
					Genesis 1:1-2:4a							
					I sing the almighty power of God	398					O	
					Let us with a gladsome mind [P]	389						
					Many and great, O God, are thy works	385				128		
					Most High, omnipotent, good Lord	406,407						
					Most Holy God, the Lord of heaven	31,32						
					O blest Creator, source of light (1-4)	27,28						
					Genesis 7:1-5, 11-18; 8:6-18; 9:8-13							
					A mighty fortress is our God [P]	687,688						
					Eternal Father, strong to save	608						
					It rained on the earth forty days, forty nights (1,3-4)					97		
					Lord Jesus, think on me	641	798					
					Genesis 22:1-18							
					O sorrow deep!	173						
					The God of Abraham praise	401						
					Exodus 14:10-31; 15:20-21							
					And Miriam was a weaver of unique variety				15			
					Come, sing the joy of Miriam				121			
					Sing now with joy unto the Lord [Canticle]	425						
					We give thanks unto you, O God of might					98		
					When Israel was in Egypt's land	648		228				
					Wisdom freed a holy people		905		155			
					With Miriam we will dance (1,4)				16			
					Isaiah 55:1-11							
					God moves in a mysterious way	677						
					Surely it is God who saves me [Canticle]	678,679						
					Baruch 3:9-15,32-4:4							
					Even when young, I prayed for wisdom's grace		906					
					The stars declare his glory [P]	431						
					Proverbs 8:1-8; 19-21; 9:4b-6							
					Come and seek the ways of wisdom				60			
					God, you have given us power to sound	584						
					The stars declare his glory [P]	431						
					Ezekiel 36:24-28							
					As longs the deer for cooling streams [P]	658						
					As panting deer desire the waterbrooks [P]		727					
					Before thy throne, O God, we kneel	574,575						

continued on page 77

This page left blank intentionally.

						H82	WLP	LEVAS II	VF	MHSO	CG descant	Inst descant
Entrance	Sequence	Offertory	Communion	Postcommunion								
					Ezekiel 37:1-14							
					Breath of God, life-bearing wind				59		o	
					Breathe on me, Breath of God	508						
					Go forth for God; go to the world in peace	347						
					Let it breathe on me			116				
					Put forth, O God, thy Spirit's might	521						
					Spirit of the living God			115				
					Zephaniah 3:14-20							
					New songs of celebration render [P]	413						
					Surely it is God who saves me	678,679						
					At the Eucharist							
			▨		At the Lamb's high feast we sing [S]	174						▨
					Camina, pueblo de Dios/Walk on, O people of God [S]		739					
▨					Christ has arisen [S]			41				
▨					Christ is arisen (Christ ist erstanden) [S]	713						
▨			▨		Christ Jesus lay in death's strong bands [S]	185,186						
▨					Christ the Lord is risen again [S]	184						
▨					Christians, to the Paschal victim [S]	183						
				▨	Come, ye faithful, raise the strain [S]	199,200						
					Day of delight and beauty unbounded [S]		738					
			▨		God sent his Son, they called him Jesus [S]			43				
				▨	Jesus Christ is risen today [S]	207						▨
					Oh, how good is Christ the Lord / Oh, qué bueno es Jesús [S]					103		
					The Lamb's high banquet called to share [S]	202						
				▨	The strife is o'er, the battle done [S]	208						▨
					Romans 6:3-11							
▨					All who believe and are baptized	298						
▨					Baptized in water	294	767	121				
			▨		God's Paschal Lamb is sacrificed for us		880				o	
▨					Through the Red Sea brought at last	187						
▨					We know that Christ is raised and dies no more	296					o	
					Matthew 28:1-10							
	▨				At break of day three women came				50			
					O sons and daughters, let us sing (1-3,5)	203						
					On earth has dawned this day of days	201						
					At Baptism if after the sermon:							
					All who believe and are baptized	298						
					Baptized in water	294	767	121				
					Crashing waters at creation					95		▨
					It rained on the earth forty days, forty nights					97		
					Over the chaos of the empty waters	176,177						
					Wade in the water		740	143				
					We know that Christ is raised and dies no more	296					o	
					You have put on Christ					122		

Anthem	Solo	Handbells	Voicing		Collection	Composer
				Acts 10:34-43		
				Jeremiah 31:1-6 (alt)		
				Psalm 118:1-2, 14-24		
✓				Confitemini Domino		Multiple
✓				Easter Antiphon		David Hurd
✓				Haec Dies		Multiple
✓				Haec es Dies		Multiple
✓				This Day		Marvin Curtis
✓				This Is the Day		Multiple
				Colossians 3:1-4		
	✓			Awake All Ye People, *Cantata 15*	LIFT	J S Bach
				Acts 10:34-43 (alt)		
				John 20:1-18		
✓				Alleluia		Multiple
			SSA	O filii et filiae		F A Gevaert
			SSAATTBB			V Leising
				Regina caeli		Multiple
				Victimae paschali laudes		Multiple
✓				Alleluia		Multiple
	✓		Soprano	I Know That My Redeemer..., *Messiah*		G F Handel
				Additional Music		
✓				Alleluia (2)	BFAS	J S Bach
						Randall Thompson
						David Ashley White
				Alleluia, *Coronation Anthem No 2 and 3*		G F Handel
			2 pt treble, inst	All Shall Be Well		Libby Larsen
				Angels Rolled the Stone Away		arr Jester Hairston
				Benedicamus Domino		Multiple
				Blessed Art Thou, O..., *All Night Vigil*		Sergei Rachmaninoff
				Christ Jesus Lay in Death's Strong...		J S Bach
		✓	2 pt mixed, tabor	Easter Sequence, Victimae..., *The Pilgrim*		Richard Proulx
			brass, opt choir	Entrata Festiva		Flor Peeters
				Festival Alleluias		Wm Ferris/C-M Widor
				Gloria		Marvin Curtis
				Hallelujah, *Messiah*		G F Handel
				Low in the Grave He Lay		M Roger Holland
				Mighty Day		Marvin Curtis
				Today Hath Salvation..., *All Night Vigil*		Sergei Rachmaninoff
				When Thou, O Lord..., *All Night Vigil*		Sergei Rachmaninoff
				We Have Seen Thy..., *All Night Vigil*		Sergei Rachmaninoff
✓				Ye Choirs of New Jerusalem	AFC 1	Charles V Stanford
	✓		Soprano	Alleluia		W A Mozart
				Cantatas/Major Works		
				4: Christ lag in Todes Banden		J S Bach
				31: Der Himmel lacht! die Erde jubilieret		J S Bach
				Easter Oratorio		J S Bach

Entrance	Sequence	Offertory	Communion	Postcommunion		H82	WLP	LEVAS II	VF	MHSO	CG descant	Inst descant
				X	Amen [S]			233				
		X			At the Lamb's high feast we sing [S]	174						X
	X				Christ has arisen [S]			41		100		
			X		Christ is arisen / Christ ist erstanden [S]	713						
	X				Christ is risen from the dead [S]		816,817					
	X				Christ Jesus lay in death's strong bands [S]	185,186						
X					Come, ye faithful, raise the strain [S]	199,200						
				X	Day of delight and beauty unbounded [S]		738					
X					God's Paschal Lamb is sacrificed for us [S]		880				o	
			X		Good Christians all, rejoice and sing [S]	205						
X					Jesus Christ is risen today [S]	207						X
	X				Look there! the Christ our brother comes [S]	196,197						
			X		Sing hallelujah to the Lord [S]				115			
			X		The Lamb's high banquet called to share [S]	202						
		X			The strife is o'er, the battle done [S]	208						X
	X				This is the day that the Lord hath made [P]		219					
					Acts 10:34-43							
X					Hail thee, festival day	175					X	X
	X				In Christ there is no East or West	529		62			X	
		X			Sing, ye faithful, sing with gladness	492						
X					"Welcome, happy morning!" age to age shall say	179						X
					Jeremiah 31:1-6							
	X				Awake and sing the song	181						
			X		Come away to the skies	213						
			X		Great is thy faithfulness, O God my Father			189				X
		X			O Zion, tune thy voice	543						
			X		Thou hallowed chosen morn of praise	198						
					Colossians 3:1-4							
		X			Alleluia, alleluia! Hearts and voices heavenward raise	191					X	
X					Love's redeeming work is done	188,189						
X				X	The day of resurrection	210						X
			X		We know that Christ is raised and dies no more	296					o	
					John 20:1-18							
	X				Apostle of the Word				13			
	X				Christ the Lord is risen again	184						
	X				Christians, to the Paschal victim	183						
			X		I come to the garden alone			69				
X					Lift your voice rejoicing, Mary	190						
					Myrrh-bearing Mary from Magdala came				2			
					That Easter morn at break of day				45	99		
		X		X	They crucified my Savior			40				
					Matthew 28:1-10							
	X				At break of day three women came				50			
	X				O sons and daughters, let us sing (1-3,5)	203						
	X				On earth has dawned this day of days	201						

o Same tune, but not text [S] Seasonal [C] Collect [P] Psalm [GR] Gospel-related [SC] Semi-continuous

Anthem	Solo	Handbells	Voicing		Collection	Composer
				Isaiah 25:6-9		
■				Festival Canticle: This Is the Feast		Peter Hallock
■						Richard Hillert
■						Mark Mummert
■				O sacrum convivium *ed. with alleluias*		Multiple
■				O Sacred Communion		Larry Long
■				O Sacred Feast		Healey Willan
				Psalm 114		
■				In exitu Israel		Antonio Vivaldi
■				Psalm 114		Zoltan Kodaly
■				When Israel Came Out..., In exitu Israel		William Byrd
■			SATB/SATB			Samuel Wesley
■				When Israel Went Out of Egypt		H L Hassler
				1 Corinthians 5:6b-8		
■				Christ Our Passover		Richard Dirksen
■						Will C MacFarlane
■	■			Christ lag in Todes Banden, *Cantata 4*		J S Bach
				Luke 24:13-49		
■				Come, Risen Lord	Aug ChB	John Bertalot
■				I Believe This Is Jesus	Aug ChB	Spiritual, arr Undine Smith Moore
■				O Paschal Lamp of Radiant Light	Aug ChB	Sam Batt Owens
■				O Sacred Communion		Larry Long
■				O Sacred Feast		Healey Willan
■				O sacrum convivium *editions with alleluias*		Multiple
■			SATB, Vla	Who Is This?		John Ferguson
■	■			Bleib bei uns, denn es will..., *Cantata 6*		J S Bach
■	■			Erfreut euch, ihr Herzen, *Cantata 66*		J S Bach
				Additional Music		
■				Phos hilaron		Multiple
				Cantatas/Major Works		
				4: Christ lag in Todes Banden		J S Bach
				6: Bleib bei uns, denn es will Abend werden		J S Bach
				66: Erfreut euch, ihr Herzen		J S Bach
				158: Der Friede sei mit dir		J S Bach

Entrance	Sequence	Offertory	Communion	Postcommunion		H82	WLP	LEVAS II	VF	MHSO	CG descant	Inst descant
	■				Christ has arisen [S]			41		100		
	■		■		Christ is arisen / Christ ist erstanden [S]	713						
					Christ is risen from the dead [S]		816,817					
				■	Day of delight and beauty unbounded [S]		738					
		■		■	Good Christians all, rejoice and sing [S]	205						
■				■	Jesus Christ is risen today [S]	207					■	■
	■				Look there! the Christ our brother comes [S]	196,197						
	■				The strife is o'er, the battle done [S]	208						■
					Isaiah 25:6-9							
	■				This is the feast of victory for our God	417,418						
			■		This is the hour of banquet and of song	316,317						
					1 Corinthians 5:6b-8							
■					At the Lamb's high feast we sing	174						■
		■			Christ Jesus lay in death's strong bands	185,186						
	■				Christ the Lord is risen again	184						
■					God's Paschal Lamb is sacrificed for us		880				O	
			■		The Lamb's high banquet called to share	202						
					Luke:24:13-49							
	■				As we gather at your Table		763				O	
			■		Come, risen Lord, and deign to be our guest	305,306						
■					Come, ye faithful, raise the strain	199,200						
	■				O sons and daughters, let us sing	203						
			■		Shepherd of souls, refresh and bless	343					■	
				■	That Easter day with joy was bright	193					■	

This page left blank intentionally.

						H82	WLP	LEVAS II	VF	MHSO	CG descant	Inst descant
Entrance	Sequence	Offertory	Communion	Postcommunion								

MONDAY IN EASTER WEEK

Position	Hymn	H82	WLP	LEVAS II	VF	MHSO	CG descant	Inst descant
Sequence	Alleluia, alleluia! Hearts and voices heavenward raise [S]	191					■	
Sequence	Christ is arisen / Christ ist erstanden [S]	713						
	Jesus is Lord of all the earth [S]	178						■
Communion	O Love of God, how strong and true [S]	455,456					■	
	This is the day that the Lord hath made [P]			219				

Acts 2:14,22b-32

Position	Hymn	H82	WLP	LEVAS II	VF	MHSO	CG descant	Inst descant
Entrance	Christ the Lord is risen again	184						
Entrance	Good Christians all, rejoice and sing	205						
Offertory	Jesus lives! thy terrors now	194,195					■	
	Sing, ye faithful, sing with gladness	492						

Matthew 28:9-15

Position	Hymn	H82	WLP	LEVAS II	VF	MHSO	CG descant	Inst descant
Entrance	Awake, arise, lift up your voice	212					■	
Entrance	Come, ye faithful, raise the strain	199,200						
Postcommunion	The day of resurrection!	210						■

TUESDAY IN EASTER WEEK

Position	Hymn	H82	WLP	LEVAS II	VF	MHSO	CG descant	Inst descant
Sequence	The whole bright world rejoices now [S]	211						
	This is the day that the Lord hath made [P]			219				

Acts 2:36-41

Position	Hymn	H82	WLP	LEVAS II	VF	MHSO	CG descant	Inst descant
Entrance	All who believe and are baptized	298						
Entrance	Baptized in water	294	767	121				
	Over the chaos of the empty waters	176,177						
Communion	The head that once was crowned with thorns	483						
Offertory	We know that Christ is raised and dies no more	296					O	

John 20:11-18

Position	Hymn	H82	WLP	LEVAS II	VF	MHSO	CG descant	Inst descant
Sequence	Apostle of the Word				13			
Entrance	Christ the Lord is risen again	184						
Offertory	Christians, to the Paschal Victim	183						
	Lift your voice rejoicing, Mary	190						
	Myrrh-bearing Mary from Magdala came				2			
	That Easter morn at break of day				45	99		
Communion	The first one ever, oh, ever to know	673						
	They crucified my Savior			40				

WEDNESDAY IN EASTER WEEK

Position	Hymn	H82	WLP	LEVAS II	VF	MHSO	CG descant	Inst descant
Sequence	Christ has arisen [S]			41		100		
Sequence	Christ is arisen / Christ ist erstanden [S]	713						
Entrance	Day of delight and beauty unbounded [S]		738					
	Good Christians all, rejoice and sing! [S]	205						
	Jesus is Lord of all the earth [S]	178						■
	This is the day that the Lord hath made [P]			219				

Acts 3:1-10

Position	Hymn	H82	WLP	LEVAS II	VF	MHSO	CG descant	Inst descant
Entrance	The fleeting day is nearly gone (1-2,4)	23						

Luke 24:13-35

Position	Hymn	H82	WLP	LEVAS II	VF	MHSO	CG descant	Inst descant
Communion	As we gather at your Table		763				O	
	Bless now, O God the journey that all your people make					142		
Communion	Come, risen Lord, and deign to be our guest	305,306						
Entrance	He is risen, he is risen!	180						
Postcommunion	Shepherd of souls, refresh and bless	343						

O Same tune, but not text   [S] Seasonal   [C] Collect   [P] Psalm   [GR] Gospel-related   [SC] Semi-continuous

This page left blank intentionally.

	Entrance / Sequence / Offertory / Communion / Postcommunion	H82	WLP	LEVAS II	VF	MHSO	CG descant	Inst descant
THURSDAY IN EASTER WEEK								
	Christ is arisen / Christ ist erstanden [S]	713						
	Oh Lord, how perfect is your name [P]			57				
	O Love of God, how strong and true [S]	455,456					■	
	The strife is o'er, the battle done [S]	208						■
	Acts 3:11-26							
	Awake and sing the song	181						
	Glorious the day when Christ was born	452						
	Sing, ye faithful, sing with gladness	492					■	
	Luke 24:36b-48							
	Awake, arise, lift up your voice	212					■	
	Come, ye faithful, raise the strain	199,200						
	Look, there! the Christ our brother comes	196,197						
	O sons and daughters, let us sing	203						
	That Easter day with joy was bright	193					■	
FRIDAY IN EASTER WEEK								
	Christ Jesus lay in death's strong bands [S]	185,186						
	Christ the Lord is risen again [S]	184						
	He is risen, he is risen! [S]	180						
	Jesus lives! thy terrors now [S]	194,195						
	This is the day that the Lord hath made [P]			219				
	Acts 4:1-12							
	Christ is made the sure foundation	518					■	
	O love, how deep, how broad, how high	448,449					■	
	To the Name of our salvation	248,249						
	John 21:1-14							
	Come, risen Lord, and deign to be our guest	305,306						
	I come with joy to meet my Lord	304					■	
	O Food to pilgrims given	308,309						
SATURDAY IN EASTER WEEK								
	Christ is alive! Let Christians sing	182						■
	Jesus lives! thy terrors now	194,195						
	The Lamb's high banquet called to share	202						
	The whole bright world rejoices now [S]	211						
	This is the day that the Lord hath made [P]			219				
	This joyful Eastertide [S]	192						
	Acts 4:13-21							
	Lord, speak to me that I may speak				98			
	Mark 16:9-15,20							
	Apostle of the Word				13			
	Christians, to the Pascal victim	183						
	Lift your voice rejoicing, Mary	190						
	Sing, ye faithful, sing with gladness	492					■	
	The first one ever, oh, ever to know	673						
	Ye servants of God, your Master proclaim	535						

Anthem	Solo	Handbells	Voicing		Collection	Composer
				Acts 2:14a, 22-32		
■			SAB	Awake, my Heart, with Gladness		Jane Marshall
■				The One Who Died by Sinners' Hands		Christopher Tye, ed Schalk
				When Thou, O Lord, Hadst..., *All Night Vigil*		Sergei Rachmaninoff
■	■		Tenor	Thou Didst Not Leave His Soul in Hell, *Messiah*		G F Handel
				Psalm 16		
■				I Have Set the Lord Always Before Me		Carl Schalk
■				O Lord You Are My Portion and My Cup		Jack Noble White
■				All the Ways of a Man		Knut Nystedt
■				Preserve Me, O Lord		Paul Manz
			Tenor	Thou Didst Not Leave His Soul in Hell, *Messiah*		G F Handel
				1 Peter 1:3-9		
■				Blessed be the God and Father	OXCAB	Samuel Wesley
			SSB or SS, 2 vn	Gelobet sei Gott		G P Telemann
				John 20:19-31		
■				Although the Doors Were Closed		James Clemens
				Benedicamus Domino		Multiple
■				Come, Risen Lord	AUG	John Bertalot
				Come You Faithful, Raise the Strain	OXEA	R S Thatcher
				Dona nobis pacem, *Mass in B Minor*		J S Bach
■				Easter Morning, O Peace Be Unto You	AUG	Paul Christiansen
■			SATB, T solo	Grieve Not the Holy Spirit		T Tertius Noble
				I Believe This Is Jesus	AUG	Spiritual, arr Undine Smith Moore
				Lauda Sion		Multiple
			SSATBB	Mitte manum tuam		Gerald Near
			SSA	O filii et filiae		F A Gevaert
			SSAATTBB			V Leising
				O Paschal Lamp of Radiant Light	AUG	Sam Batt Owens
				O Sacred Communion		Larry Long
				O Sacred Feast		Healey Willan
				O sacrum convivium *editions with Alleluias*		Multiple
				Peace, Perfect Peace		Libby Larsen
				Peace Be Unto You		Knut Nystedt
			2 pt	Peace Be with You		Jan Bender
						Bruce Neswick
				Quia vidisti me		Hans Leo Hassler
						Luca Marenzio
						G P Palestrina
				Real, Jesus Is Real to Me		Beatrice Brown
				Receive the Holy Spirit		Richard Hillert
				Stetit Jesus, Then Stood Jesus		Jacob Handl
				Surgens Jesus		Multiple
				When Thou, O Lord, Hadst..., *All Night Vigil*		Sergei Rachmaninoff
			SATB, vla	Who Is This?		John Ferguson
		■		O Sons and Daughters		Fred Gramann
				Additional Music		
■				Scio enim	CHES	Jacob Vaet
				This Is the Feast of Victory for Our God		Russell Schulz-Widmar
■				I Know That My Redeemer Liveth, *Messiah*		G F Handel
	■		Tenor	Thou Didst Not Leave His Soul in Hell, *Messiah*		G F Handel
				Cantatas/ Major Works		
				4: Christ lag in Todes Banden		J S Bach
				42: Am Abend aber desselbigen Sabbats		J S Bach
				67: Halt im Gedächtnis Jesum Christ		J S Bach
				158: Der Friede sei mit dir		J S Bach

	Entrance	Sequence	Offertory	Communion	Postcommunion		H82	WLP	LEVAS II	VF	MHSO	CG descant	Inst descant
						Acts 2:14a,22-32							
	▨		▨			Christ the Lord is risen again	184						
▨		▨				Good Christians all, rejoice and sing	205						
		▨				Jesus is Lord of all the earth	178						▨
	▨					Jesus lives! thy terrors now	194,195						
▨				▨		Sing, ye faithful, sing with gladness	492						
▨						This joyful Eastertide	192						
						1 Peter 1:3-9							
	▨					Glorious the day when Christ was born	452						
	▨					Hope of the world, thou Christ of great compassion	472						
						John 20:18-31							
	▨					Awake, arise, lift up your voice	212					▨	
		▨				By all your saints still striving (2: St. Thomas)	231,232					▨	
			▨			How oft, O Lord, thy face hath shone	242						
			▨			In the bulb there is a flower					86		
	▨		▨			O sons and daughters, let us sing	206						
				▨		We walk by faith and not by sight	209		206			▨	

Anthem	Solo	Handbells	Voicing		Collection	Composer
				Acts 2:14a, 36-41		
X				Shout for Joy!		John Carter
X				The Man We Crucified		Christopher Tye, ed Schalk
X				When Thou, O Lord, Hadst…, *All Night Vigil*		Sergei Rachmaninoff
				Psalm 116:1-4, 12-19		
X				I Love the Lord		Richard Smallwood
X			SAB	My Delight Is in the Lord		Robert J Powell
X				Return Unto Thy Rest		Jean Pasquet
X			TTB	Since God So Tender a Regard		Henry Purcell
X			2 pt	What Shall I Render to My God		Austin Lovelace
				1 Peter 1:17-23		
X				Blessed be the God and Father	OXCAB	Samuel Wesley
X			Unison	Love One Another		Samuel Wesley
				Luke 24:13-35		
X			2 pt	Alleluia! Risen Indeed		Roger Petrich
X				And They Drew Nigh		Leo Sowerby
X			SAB	Christ Who Alone Art Light of Day		Hugo Distler
X				Cognoverunt discipuli		William Byrd
X				Come, Risen Lord	AUG	John Bertalot
X				I Believe This Is Jesus	AUG	Spiritual, arr Undine Smith Moore
X				Lauda Sion		Multiple
X				Mane nobiscum		Gerald Near
X				O Paschal Lamp of Radiant Light	AUG	Sam Batt Owens
X				O Sacred Communion		Larry Long
X				O Sacred Feast		Healey Willan
X				O sacrum convivium *ed with alleluias*		Multiple
X			SATB, Vla	Who Is This?		John Ferguson
X		X		Bleib bei uns, denn es will…, *Cantata 6*		J S Bach
X		X		Erfreut euch, ihr Herzen, *Cantata 66*		J S Bach
				Additional Music		
X		X		Ring Out Your Joy		Harrison Oxley
X				Scio enim	CHES	Jacob Vaet
X				This Is the Feast of Victory for Our God		Russell Schulz-Widmar
X				Christ lag in Todes Banden		J S Bach
	X		Soprano	I Know That My Redeemer Liveth, *Messiah*		G F Handel

Entrance	Sequence	Offertory	Communion	Postcommunion		H82	WLP	LEVAS II	VF	MHSO	CG descant	Inst descant
					Acts 2:14a,36-41							
	X				All who believe and are baptized	298						
	X				Baptized in water	294	767	121				
	X				Over the chaos of the empty waters	176,177						
X					The head that once was crowned with thorns	483						
		X		X	We know that Christ is raised and dies no more	296					o	
					1 Peter 1:17-23							
	X				Hail, thou once despised Jesus!	495						X
	X				Lord, enthroned in heavenly splendor	307						
X		X			Now the green blade riseth	204						
	X	X			This is the feast of victory for our God	417,418						
					Luke 24:13-35							
			X		As we gather at your Table		763				o	
			X		Come, risen Lord, and deign to be our guest	305,306						X
X					He is risen, he is risen!	180						X
			X	X	Shepherd of souls, refresh and bless	343					X	

o Same tune, but not text [S] Seasonal [C] Collect [P] Psalm [GR] Gospel-related [SC] Semi-continuous

Anthem	Solo	Handbells	Voicing		Collection	Composer
				Acts 2:42-47		
				Draw Us in the Spirit's Tether		Harold Friedell
				Lauda Sion		Multiple
				Psalm 23		
				Brother James' Air		Gordon Jacob
				Flocks in Pastures Green Abiding	OXEA	J S Bach
				Lauda Sion		Multiple
				My Shepherd Is Lord		Harrison Oxley
			2 pt	No More a Stranger or a Guest		David Ashley White
				Psalm 23		Multiple
				The Lord Is My Shepherd		Howard Goodall
				The Lord My Shepherd		David Ashley White
				The Lord Is My Shepherd, *Requiem*		John Rutter
				The Lord Is My Shepherd	LIFT	Peter Pindar Stearns
				1 Peter 2:19-25		
				Agnus Dei		Multiple
				And with His Stripes, *Messiah*		G F Handel
				All We Like Sheep, *Messiah*		G F Handel
				Also hat Gott die Welt geliebet		Gallus Dressler
				And with His Stripes, *Messiah*		G F Handel
				Behold the Lamb of God		J Brahms
				Behold the Lamb of God, *Messiah*		G F Handel
				Furwahr! Er trug unsre..., Surely He Hath		Carl Heinrich Graun
						Hugo Distler
				God Remembers		Russell Schulz-Widmar
			2 pt	God Sent His Son into the World		G F Handel
				He That Shall Endure to the End, *Elijah*		Felix Mendelssohn
				Salvation Unto Us Has Come		J S Bach
				Since by Man Came Death, *Messiah*		G F Handel
				Since by Man Came Death	SEW	Thomas Pavlechko
				Surely He Hath Borne Our Griefs, *Messiah*		G F Handel
				Weinen, Klagen, Sorgen, Zagen, *Cantata 12*		J S Bach
				Wir müssen durch viel Trübsal, *Cantata 146*		J S Bach
				John 10:1-10		
				All We Like Sheep, *Messiah*		G F Handel
			2 pt	I Am the Good Shepherd		Jan Bender
						Austin Lovelace
						Alice Parker
				Lauda Zion		Multiple
				Listen to the Lambs		arr R Nathaniel Dett
				O quam gloriosum	CHES	Jacob Vaet
				Surrexit a mortuis		Charles-Marie Widor
				Surrexit pastor bonus		Multiple
			2 pt	The Good Shepherd		Anna Laura Page
				These Are They Which Follow the Lamb	AFC 1	John Goss
				Victimae paschali laudes		Various
				Er rufet seinen Schafen..., *Cantata 175*		J S Bach
				Erwünschtes Freudenlicht, *Cantata 184*		J S Bach
				Cantatas/Major Works		
				112: Der Herr ist mein getreuer Hirt		J S Bach

Entrance	Sequence	Offertory	Communion	Postcommunion		H82	WLP	LEVAS II	VF	MHSO	CG descant	Inst descant
▨				▨	Good Christians all, rejoice and sing! (1,3-5) [S]	205						
			▨		My Shepherd will supply my need [P]	664						▨
			▨		The King of love my shepherd is [P]	645,646					▨	
			▨		The Lord is my Shepherd [P]			104				
			▨		The Lord my God my Shepherd is [P]	663						
					The Lord, the Lord, the Lord is my shepherd [P]					102		
			▨		You are my shepherd [P]					104		
					Acts 2:42-47							
▨					Come now, O Prince of Peace, make us one body		795					
▨					I come with joy to meet my Lord	304					▨	
					1 Peter 2:19-25							
▨		▨			Christ the Lord is risen again	184						
		▨			Shepherd of souls, refresh and bless	343					▨	
▨		▨			Sing, ye faithful, sing with gladness	492						
		▨			The strife is o'er, the battle done	208						▨
					John 10:1-10							
				▨	Jesus, our mighty Lord	478						
				▨	Praise the Lord, rise up rejoicing	334						
				▨	Savior, like a shepherd lead us	708						▨

Anthem	Solo	Handbells	Voicing		Collection	Composer
				Collect		
●				Come My Way, My Truth My Life		Harold Friedell
	●		Baritone	The Call, *Five Mystical Songs*		Ralph Vaughan Williams
				Acts 7:55-60		
●				O Salutaris Hostia		Multiple
●			SATB, T solo	Stephen		Alec Wyton
●			SSAATBB	Stephen Being Full of the Holy Ghost		Thomas Tomkins
				Psalm 31:1-5 15-16		
●				In te, Domine		Josquin des Prez
●						Heinrich Schütz
●			SATTB	In te speravi		G P Palestrina
●				In Thee O Lord		Thomas Weelkes
●			Unison	In Thee O Lord Do I Put My Trust		Jan Bender
●				In Thee, O Lord, Have I Trusted	CON	G F Handel
●			Unison	Let Your Face Shine		Richard Wienhorst
●				O How Amiable		Ralph Vaughan Williams
	●		Alto	In deine Hände befehl ich..., *Cantata 106*		J S Bach
				1 Peter 2:2-10		
●				At the Name of Jesus		Ralph Vaughan Williams
●				Christ is Made the Sure Foundation		Dale Wood
●				God's Own People		Jane Marshall
●				O Taste and See		Ralph Vaughan Williams
				John 14:1-14		
●				Alleluia for a Festival		David Hurd
●				At the Name of Jesus		Ralph Vaughan Williams
●				Come My Way, My Truth, My Life		Harold Friedell
●				How Lovely Is Thy Dwelling Place, *Requiem*		Johannes Brahms
●				In This House		Richard Smallwood
●				Let Not Your Heart Be Troubled		Carl F Mueller
●						Robert J Powell
●				O How Amiable		Ralph Vaughan Williams
●			SSA, SA solos	Peace I Leave with You		Will C MacFarlane
●				The House of Faith Has Many Rooms		Craig Phillips
●				You Are the Way		David Ashley White
	●			O Christ, the Way	LIFT	Felix Mendelssohn
	●			Plenty Good Room	SOS	Spiritual, arr Boatner
			Baritone	The Call, *Five Mystical Songs*		Ralph Vaughan Williams
				Additional Music		
●				Awake, My Heart, With Gladness		Jane Marshall
●				Scio enim	CHES	Jacob Vaet
	●		Soprano	I Know That My Redeemer Liveth, *Messiah*		G F Handel
				Cantatas/Major Works		
●				229: Komm, Jesu, Komm! (motet)		J S Bach

Entrance	Sequence	Offertory	Communion	Postcommunion		H82	WLP	LEVAS II	VF	MHSO	CG descant	Inst descant
				■	Come away to the skies [S]	213						
					Acts 7:55-60							
	■				When Stephen full of power and grace	243						
	■				By all your saints still striving (St. Stephen)	231,232					■	
					1 Peter 2:2-10							
■	■				Christ is made the sure foundation	518					■	
■	■				Open your ears, O faithful people	536						
	■				God of the prophets	359						
■				■	The Church's one foundation	525					■	■
■					We the Lord's people, heart and voice uniting	51					■	■
	■				When from bondage we are summoned		753,754					■
					John 14:1-14							
			■		Come, my Way, my Truth, my Life	487						
■					Father, we praise thee, now the night is over	1,2						
			■		He is the Way	463,464						
			■		Here, O Lord, your servants gather		793					
		■			Praise the Lord through every nation	484,485						
				■	Thou art the Way, to thee alone	457						

Anthem	Solo	Handbells	Voicing		Collection	Composer
				Acts 17:22-31		
				All Have a God Whom They Revere		Christopher Tye, ed Schalk
				Gottes Zeit ist die allerbeste Zeit, *Cantata 106*		J S Bach
				Laus Trinitati		Frank Ferko
				O Come Hither	AFC 2	Maurice Greene
				Psalm 66:7-18		
				Jubilate Deo (Ps 100)		Multiple
				O Be Joyful		Multiple
			SS	O Come Hither	AFC 2	Maurice Greene
			SSATB	O Come Hither and Harken		John Amner
				1 Peter 3:13-22		
				Agnus Dei		Multiple
				All Who Believe and Are Baptized	BFAS	J S Bach
				And with His Stripes, *Messiah*		G F Handel
				Behold the Lamb of God		J Brahms
				Behold the Lamb of God, *Messiah*		G F Handel
				God Remembers		Russell Schulz-Widmar
				He That Shall Endure to the End, *Elijah*		Felix Mendelssohn
				Laus Trinitati		Frank Ferko
				Salvation Unto Us Has Come		J S Bach
				Since by Man Came Death, *Messiah*		G F Handel
				Since by Man Came Death	SEW	Thomas Pavlechko
				Wer nur den lieben Gott lässt..., *Cantata 93*		J S Bach
				Worthy Is the Lord		William Murphy Jr & Shannon Davis
	Soprano			If God Be for Us, *Messiah*		G F Handel
				John 14:15-21		
			SSA or SSAA	If Ye Love Me		Harvey B Gaul
			SSA			Daniel Pinkham
						Thomas Tallis
			SSA			Healey Willan
						Philip Wilby
				I Will Not Leave You Comfortless, SSATB		William Byrd
			2 pt			Ron Nelson
						Everett Titcomb
				My Peace I Give		Antonio Lotti
			SSATB or TTBB	Non vos relinquam orphanos		William Byrd
				O rex gloriae	CHES	Luca Marenzio
				Peace I Leave with You		Knut Nystedt
						Walter Pelz
				Shout for Joy!		John Carter
				Scio enim	CHES	Orlando Lassus
	Soprano			I Know That My Redeemer Liveth, *Messiah*		G F Handel
				Additional Music		
				Ye Servants of God	OXEA	arr Henry Coleman
				Cantatas/Major Works		
				108: Es ist euch gut, dass ich hingehe		J S Bach

Entrance	Sequence	Offertory	Communion	Postcommunion		H82	WLP	LEVAS II	VF	MHSO	CG descant	Inst descant
■				■	Alleluia, alleluia! Hearts and voices heavenward raise [S]	191					■	■
		■			As those of old their first fruits brought [Rogation]	705					■	■
■					Now the green blade riseth [S]	204						
				■	O Jesus, crowned with all renown [Rogation]	292						
					Acts 17:22-31							
		■			All things bright and beautiful	405			111,112			
		■			Cantemos al Señor / O sing unto the Lord					134		
	■				Creating God, your fingers trace	394,395						
			■		Creator of all time and space				102			
					God of the sparrow God of the whale					129		
					God the sculptor of the mountains		746,747			130		
					Heaven and earth, join to worship your Creator					133		
		■			Let all things now living				107			
	■				Many and great, O God, are thy works	385				128		
			■		This is my Father's world	651						
			■		We are a part of all creation					131		
		■			We plow the fields and scatter	291						
■					We sing of God, the mighty source	386,387						
					1 Peter 3:13-22							
■		■		■	O Love of God, how strong and true	455,456					■	
■	■	■		■	Sing, ye faithful, sing with gladness	492					■	
					John 14:15-21							
	■				Come down, O Love divine	516					■	
	■				Come gracious Spirit, heavenly Dove	512						
			■		Creator Spirit, by whose aid	500						
					I serve a risen Savior			42				
			■		More love to thee, O Christ			87				
			■		O thou who camest from above	704						
		■			To thee, O Comforter divine	514						

Anthem	Solo	Handbells	Voicing		Collection	Composer
				Collect		
●				O God the King of Glory		Orlando Gibbons
				Acts 1:1-11		
●			SSATB	Men of Galilee		J P Sweelinck
				The Parting Word the Savior Spoke		Christopher Tye, ed Schalk
				Viri Galilaei		William Byrd
					CHES	Couillart
	●			Lobet Gott in seinen..., *Ascension Oratorio*		J S Bach
				Psalm 47		
●				Ascendit Deus		Multiple
				Clap Hands All People, *Bay Psalm Book*		Jean Berger
				Clap Your Hands		René Clausen
			2 pt, perc			Peter Hallock
						John P Kee
			SSAATB	God Is Gone Up with a Merry Noise		William Croft
						Herbert Howells
				Laudate Dominum in sanctis ejus		Multiple
			SA or SAB	O Clap Your Hands		F Couperin, arr Jewell
			SSAATTBB		TUD	Orlando Gibbons
			2 pt			John Horman
						William Mathias
			2 pt			Robert J Powell
						John Rutter
						Ralph Vaughan Williams
				Psalm 93 (alt)		
●				Dominus regnat		Knut Nystedt
				God Omnipotent Reigneth		Pierre Dacques
				King's Daughters, *Coronation Anthem No 4*		G F Handel
				Psalm 93		Heinrich Schütz
				The Lord Is King		Leo Sowerby
			2 pt.	The Lord Shall Reign		David Hurd
				Upon Thy Right Hand, *Coron. Anthem No 4*		G F Handel
				Ephesians 1:15-23		
●				At the Name of Jesus		Ralph Vaughan Williams
				Beautiful Savior		F. Melius Christiansen
	●		SAB			Russell Schulz-Widmar
	●		Bass	Thou Art Gone Up on High, *Messiah*		G F Handel
				Luke 24:44-53		
●				Glory and Worship, *Coron. Anthem No 3*		G F Handel
				Lift Up Your Heads	16th	John Amner
				Lift Up Your Heads, *Messiah*		G F Handel
				Lift Up Your Heads		William Mathias
				O God the King of Glory	AFC 1	Henry Purcell
				O Rex gloriae	CHES	Luca Marenzio
				The Ascension		Philip Moore
	●			Lobet Gott in seinen..., *Ascension Oratorio*		J S Bach
				Cantatas/Major Works		
				37: Wer da gläubet und getauft wird		J S Bach
				43: Gott fähret auf mit Jauchzen		J S Bach
				128: Auf Christi Himmelfahrt allein		J S Bach

						H82	WLP	LEVAS II	VF	MHSO	CG descant	Inst descant
					And have the bright immensities [S]	459						
		▓			Clap your hands, all you people [P]					113		
					"Go preach my gospel," saith the Lord [S]			161				
▓					Hail thee, festival day! [S]	216						▓
					Acts 1:1-11							
	▓				A hymn of glory let us sing	217,218						▓
▓			▓		Alleluia! sing to Jesus!	460,461						▓
▓					Hail the day that sees him rise	214						
		▓			See, the Conqueror mounts in triumph	215						
					The Lord ascendeth up on high	219						
					Ephesians 1:15-23							
	▓				Crown him with many crowns	494						▓
		▓			Emmanuel! The angels' ancient chorus				46			
▓					Hail, thou once despised Jesus	495						▓
		▓			He is king of kings, he is Lord of lords			96				
					It was poor little Jesus, yes, yes	468						
		▓			Lord, enthroned in heavenly splendor	307						
					O Lord most high, eternal King	220,221						
					Rejoice, the Lord is King	481						
					Rejoice, the Lord of life ascends	222						
					We see the Lord					114		
					Luke 24:44-53							
	▓				A hymn of glory let us sing	217,218						
▓	▓				Alleluia! sing to Jesus!	460,461						▓
▓					Hail the day that sees him rise	214						
		▓			See, the Conqueror mounts in triumph	215						
			▓		The Lord ascendeth up on high	219						

Anthem	Solo	Handbells	Voicing		Collection	Composer
				Collect		
				O God, the King of Glory		Orlando Gibbons
					AFC 1	Henry Purcell
				Acts 1:6-14		
				Going Up Yonder		Walter Hawkins
			SSATB	Men of Galilee		J P Sweelinck
				The Parting Word the Savior Spoke		Christopher Tye, ed Schalk
				Viri Galilaei		William Byrd
					CHES	Couillart
				Lobet Gott in seinen…, *Ascension Oratorio*		J S Bach
				Psalm 68:1-10, 33-36		
				God Is Gone Up		Gerald Finzi
						Arthur Hutchings
						John McCabe
				Let God Arise		Herbert Howells
						Arthur Wills
			Unison	Psalm 68		Jane Marshall
				The Lord Gave the Word, *Messiah* (Ps. 68:11)		G F Handel
				We Have Heard with Our Ears		Herbert Howells
			Bass	Thou Art Gone Up On High (Ps. 68:18)		G F Handel
				1 Peter 4:12-14; 5:6-11		
			Unison, 2 pt	A Prayer of St. Richard of Chichester	OXEA	L J White
				He That Is Down Need Fear No Fall		Philip Moore
						Ralph Vaughan Williams
			Tenor	Every Valley, *Messiah*		G F Handel
				John 17:1-11		
				Glory and Worship, *Coronation Anthem No 3*		G F Handel
				I Have Known You		Thomas Keesecker
				Look, Oh Look, the Sight is Glorious		S Drummond Wolff
				Additional Music		
				Ascendit Deus		Multiple
				Draw Us in the Spirit's Tether		Harold Friedell
				God Is Gone Up with a Merry Noise		Herbert Howells
				Lift Up Your Heads	16th	John Amner
				Lift Up Your Heads, *Messiah*		G F Handel
				Lift Up Your Heads		William Mathias
				O Word, that Goest Forth on High		David Ashley White
				O Verbum Patris, *The Hildegard Motets*		Frank Ferko
				The Ascension		Philip Moore
				Cantatas/Major Works		
				43: Gott fähret auf mit Jauchzen		J S Bach
				128: Auf Christi Himmelfahrt allein		J S Bach
				Singet dem Herrn ein neuces Lied (motet)		J S Bach

Entrance	Sequence	Offertory	Communion	Postcommunion		H82	WLP	LEVAS II	VF	MHSO	CG descant	Inst descant
■		■		■	All hail the power of Jesus' name [S]	450,451					■	
					Crown him with many crowns [S]	494					■	
					"Go preach my gospel," saith the Lord [S]			161				
		■			Praise the Lord through every nation [S]	484,485						
■		■		■	Rejoice the Lord is King [S]	481						
					Acts 1:6-14							
■		■		■	Alleluia! sing to Jesus!	460,461					■	
	■		■		Hail, thou once despised Jesus	495						■
			■		Lord, enthroned in heavenly splendor	307						
					1 Peter 4:12-14; 5:6-11							
				■	Christ is alive! Let Christians sing	182						■
		■			If thou but trust in God to guide thee	635						
■			■		No saint on earth lives life to self alone		776					
	■				Rejoice, the Lord of life ascends	222						
			■		The church of Christ in every age		779				■	
	■				The head that once was crowned with thorns	483						
					John 17:1-11							
■					Come now, O Prince of peace		795					
			■		Thou, who at thy first Eucharist didst pray	315						
			■		Unidos, unidos / Together, together		796					
		■			We are all one in mission		778				■	

Anthem	Solo	Handbells	Voicing		Collection	Composer
				Collect		
■				Draw Us in the Spirit's Tether		Harold Friedell
				Genesis 11:1-9		
				Psalm 33:12-22		
■				Exultate justi		Multiple
■				O How Amiable		Ralph Vaughan Williams
■				Our Soul Waits for the Lord		Jane Marshall
■				We Wait for Thy Loving Kindness		William McKee
				Exodus 19:1-9A, 16-20A; 20:18-20 (alt)		
■				Ev'ry Time I Feel the Spirit		arr William Dawson
■				On Eagle's Wings		Michael Joncas
■				Tuba mirum		Multiple
	■			On Eagle's Wings		Michael Joncas
				Canticle 2 or 13 (w/Exodus)		
■				Benedicamus Domino		Multiple
■				Te Deum		Multiple
				Ezekiel 37:1-14 (alt)		
■				Dry Bones		Spiritual, Various
				Psalm 130 (w/Ezekiel)		
■				De profundis		Multiple
■				Out of the Depths		Jacques Charpentier
■				Out of the Deep, *Requiem*		John Rutter
■				Psalm 130		Multiple
■				Aus tiefer Not schrei ich zu dir, *Cantata 38*		J S Bach
■				Aus der Tiefen rufe ich, Herr..., *Cantata 131*		J S Bach
				Joel 2:28-32 alt		
■				Lo! He Comes, with Clouds Descending		David H. Williams
■			SATTB	My Lord, What a Morning		William Dawson
				Canticle 9 (w/Joel)		
■				Surely It Is God Who Saves Me		Jack Noble White
				Acts 2:1-11		
■			SAATTB	Dum complerentur dies pentecostes		G P Palestrina
■			SSATB			Tomas Luis Victoria
■				Hail, Glorious Spirits, Heirs of Light		Christopher Tye
■				In Divers Tongues		G P Palestrina
■				O Day Full of Grace		F Melius Christiansen
■			Unison	Pentecost Fire		Jayne Southwick Cool
■			SATB/SATB	Replenti sunt omnes		Jacob Handl
				Romans 8:14-17, 22-27 alt		
■				As Many As Are Led by the Spirit		David McK Williams
■				If Any Man Hath Not the Spirit		H Walford Davies
■				Like the Murmur of the Dove's Song		Peter Cutts
■				The Spirit Also Helpeth Us		J S Bach
■				Der Geist hilft unsrer Schwachhiet auf (motet)		J S Bach
				Psalm 104:25-32 (w/Acts or Romans)		
■		■	Unison	I Will Sing to the Lord As Long As I Live		Carl Schalk
■				O Taste and See		Ralph Vaughan Williams
■				Panis angelicus		Multiple
	■			Panis angelicus		César Franck
				John 7:37-39		
■				As Panting Deer Desire the Waterbrooks		David Ashley White
■				Sicut cervus		Multiple
				Additional Music		
■				Credo		Multiple
	■			The Victory of Spirit	LIFT	Franz Schubert
				Cantatas/Major Works		
				165: O heilges Geist- und Wasserbad		J S Bach

Entrance	Sequence	Offertory	Communion	Postcommunion		H82	WLP	LEVAS II	VF	MHSO	CG descant	Inst descant
					A Vigil has no entrance hymn (see BCP, pp. 175 and 227);							
					the entrance hymns suggested below are for an Early Service.							
		■			Come down, O Love divine [S]	516					■	
		■			Come, Holy Ghost, Creator blest [S]			112				
		■			Come, Holy Ghost, our souls inspire [S]	503,504						
		■			Come, Holy Spirit, descend on us [S]					108		
	■				Come, thou Holy Spirit bright [trad. Sequence]	226,227						
		■			Creator Spirit, by whose aid [S]	500						
■					From deepest woe I cry to thee [P 130]	151						
	■				Holy Spirit, font of light [trad. Sequence]	228						
			■		If you believe and I believe [S]		806					
			■		I'm goin'-a sing when the Spirit says sing [S]			117				
				■	Loving Spirit, loving Spirit [S]		742		51	111		
					May your loving spirit [S]					112		
		■			O Holy Spirit by whose breath [S]	501,502						
		■			O Holy Spirit, flowing light [S]				54			
		■			O Holy Spirit, root of life [S]				55			
			■		O Spirit of the living God [S]	531						
■					Out of the depths I call [P 130]	666						
		■			She sits like a bird, brooding on the waters [S]					110		
		■			Soplo de Dios viviente / Breath of the living God [S]					107		
		■			Spirit of mercy, truth, and love [S]	229						
		■			Surely it is God who saves me [Canticle 9]	678,679						
			■		There's a sweet, sweet Spirit in this place [S]			120				
				■	To thee, O Comforter divine [S]	514						
	■				Veni Sancte Spiritus [S]		832					
					Genesis 11:1-9							
	■				All my hope on God is founded	665					■	
	■				Father eternal, Ruler of creation	573						
					Exodus 19:1-9a; 20:18-20							
		■			Every time I feel the spirit		751	114				
■					God the Omnipotent! King, who ordainest	569						■
		■			Holy Ghost, dispel our sadness	515						
■					O worship the King, all glorious above	388					■	
					Ezekiel 37:1-14							
					See Fifth Sunday in Lent							
					Joel 2:28-32							
■					O day of God, draw nigh	600,601						
■		■			Praise the Spirit in creation	506,507					■	
			■		"Thy kingdom come!" on bended knee	615						
					Acts 2:1-11							
			■		A mighty sound from heaven	230						
				■	Filled with the Spirit's power, with one accord		741					
■					Hail thee, festival day!	225					■	
■					Hail this joyful day's return	223,224						
		■			Spirit divine, attend our prayers	509						
					Romans 8:14-17,22-27							
			■		Come, Holy Spirit, heavenly Dove	510					■	
					Eternal Spirit of the living Christ	698						
		■			Holy Spirit, ever living	511					o	
			■		Like the murmur of the dove's song	513						
				■	O Spirit of Life, O Spirit of God	505						
					Spirit of God, unseen as the wind				53			
					John 7:37-39a							
			■		I heard the voice of Jesus say	692						

■ Same tune, but not text   [S] Seasonal   [C] Collect   [P] Psalm   [GR] Gospel-related   [SC] Semi-continuous

Anthem	Solo	Handbells	Voicing		Collection	Composer
				Acts 2:1-21		
■				All People at This Hour	OXEA	J S Bach
				And in the Last Days		Emma Lou Diemer
			SAATTB	Dum complerentur dies pentecostes		G P Palestrina
			SSATB			Tomas Luis Victoria
				Ev'ry Time I Feel the Spirit		arr William Dawson
				Hail, Glorious Spirits, Heirs of Light		Christopher Tye
				Holy Spirit		Richard Smallwood
				In Divers Tongues		G P Palestrina
				O Day Full of Grace		F Melius Christiansen
			Unison	Pentecost Fire		Jayne Southwick Cool
			SATB/SATB	Replenti sunt omnes		Jacob Handl
				Numbers 11:24-30		
				Psalm 104:25-35, 37		
				How Many Are Your Works		Charles Callahan
	■		Unison	I Will Sing to the Lord As Long As I Live		Carl Schalk
				O Taste and See		Ralph Vaughan Williams
				Panis angelicus		Multiple
				The Spirit of the Lord		Charles Callahan
				1 Corinthians 12:3b-13		
				Draw Us in the Spirit's Tether		Harold Friedell
				King Jesus Hath a Garden		arr Charles Wood
				Like the Murmur of the Dove's Song		Peter Cutts
				One Bread One Body		John Foley
				Acts 2:1-21 alt		
				See above		
				John 20:19-23		
				Choral Anthems		
				Dona nobis pacem, *Mass in B Minor*, BWV232		J S Bach
				Grieve Not the Holy Spirit		T Tertius Noble
				Peace Be Unto You		Knut Nystedt
				Peace, Perfect Peace		Libby Larsen
				Stetit Jesus - Then Stood Jesus		Jacob Handl
			SATTBB	When Thou O Lord Hadst Arisen, *All Night Vigil*		Sergei Rachmaninoff
				Peace Be Unto You	LIFT	Franz Schubert
				John 7:37-39 alt		
				As Panting Deer Desire the Waterbrooks		David Ashley White
				Sicut cervus		Multiple
				Additional Music		
				Awake Us, Lord, and Hasten	AFC 1	J S Bach
				Credo		Multiple
				Ev'ry Time I Feel the Spirit		arr William Dawson
				Song 44, Veni Creator	AFC 1	Orlando Gibbons
			SSATBB	Veni Creator	CHES	Adam Rener
				We All Believe in One True God	BFAS	J S Bach
				Cantata/Major Works		
				34: O ewiges Feuer, O Ursprung…		J S Bach
				108: Es ist euch gut, dass ich hingehe		J S Bach
				165: O heilges Geist- und Wasserbad		J S Bach
	Alto, Tenor, Bass			166: Wo gehest du hin?		J S Bach
				Der Geist hilft unser…, BWV 226 (motet)		J S Bach

Entrance	Sequence	Offertory	Communion	Postcommunion		H82	WLP	LEVAS II	VF	MHSO	CG descant	Inst descant
		X			Breath of God, life-bearing wind [S]					59	O	
			X		Come down, O Love divine [S]	516					X	
			X		Come, Holy Ghost, Creator blest [S]			112			X	
			X		Come, Holy Ghost, our souls inspire [S]	503,504						
			X		Come, Holy Spirit, descend on us [S]					108		
X	X				Come, thou Holy Spirit bright [trad. Sequence]	226,227						
	X				Creator Spirit, by whose aid [S]	500						
	X				Holy Spirit, font of light [trad. Sequence]	228						
			X		If you believe and I believe [S]		806					
			X		I'm goin'-a sing when the Spirit says sing [S]			117				
		X			Loving Spirit, loving Spirit [S]		742		51	111		
			X		May your loving spirit [S]					112		
X				X	O day of radiant gladness [S]	48						X
			X		O Holy Spirit by whose breath [S]	501,502						
			X		O Holy Spirit, flowing light [S]				54			
			X		O Holy Spirit, root of life [S]				55			
			X		O Spirit of the living God [S]	531						
X				X	Praise the Spirit in creation [S]	506,507					X	
			X		She sits like a bird, brooding on the waters [S]					110		
			X		Soplo de Dios viviente / Breath of the living God [S]					107		
		X			Sprit of God, descend upon my heart [S]			119				
		X			Spirit of God, you moved over the waters [S]				58			
			X		Spirit of mercy, truth, and love [S]	229						
			X		There's a sweet, sweet Spirit in this place [S]			120				
X					This day at thy creating word [S]	52						
			X		To thee, O Comforter divine [S]	514						
	X				Veni Sancte Spiritus [S]		832					
X					We the Lord's people, heart and voice uniting [S]	51						X
Acts 2:1-21												
See Pentecost Vigil												
Numbers 11:24-30												
X					Praise to the living God!	372					O	
1 Corinthians 12:3b-13												
				X	Go forth for God; go to the world in peace	347						
X					Gracious Spirit, Holy Ghost	612						
X					Holy Spirit, Lord of love	349					O	
					I am the church! You are the church!					109		
					Lord, you give the great commission	528	780				O	
		X			O God of gentle strength		770,771				O	
		X			O thou who camest from above	704						
X					On this day, the first of days	47						
					People of God, gather together					109	O	
X					Sing praise to our Creator	295						
			X		'Tis the gift to be simple	554						
				X	We are all one in mission		778				X	
John 20:19-23												
			X		Breathe on me, Breath of God	508						
		X			Holy Spirit, ever living	511					O	
			X		Let it breathe on me			116				
John 7:37-39a												
			X		I heard the voice of Jesus say	692						
At Baptism:												
					All who believe and are baptized	298						
					Baptized in water	294	767	121				
					Descend, O Spirit, purging flame	297						
					Over the chaos of the empty waters	176,177						
					Spirit of God, unleashed on earth	299						

Anthem	Solo	Handbells	Voicing		Collection	Composer
				Genesis 1:1-2:4a		
■				Achieved Is the Glorious Work, *The Creation*		Franz Joseph Haydn
■			SSAATTBB	Bless the Lord, O My Soul, *All Night Vigil*		Sergei Rachmaninoff
■				In the Beginning		Aaron Copland
■				In the Beginning Creation		Daniel Pinkham
■				The Heavens are Telling, *The Creation*		Franz Joseph Haydn
■				The Heavens are Telling		Ludwig von Beethoven
■				When Long Before Time		David Cherwien
	■			He's Got the Whole World in His Hands		Spiritual, Various
				Psalm 8		
■			Unison	How Majestic Is Thy Name		Emma Lou Diemer
■			Unison	Lord, How Majestic Is Your Name		Austin Lovelace
■				O How Excellent Thy Name	CON 2	G F Handel
■				O Lord In Thee Do I Put My Trust		G P Palestrina
■			SSAB or SSTB	O Lord Our Governor		Henry Purcell
■			2 pt	O Lord Our Master, How Glorious...		G P Telemann
■			Unison	Psalm 8		Richard Hillert
						Heinrich Schütz
				2 Corinthians 13:11-13		
■				The Apostolic Benediction		Healey Willan
■				Ubi caritas		Maurice Duruflé
				Matthew 28:16-20		
■				Christus factus est		Multiple
■				Draw Us in the Spirit's Tether		Harold Friedell
■			SATB, Unison	Go Ye Therefore		Gerre Hancock
						Alec Wyton
				Holy, holy, holy, *Gospel Mass*		Robert Ray
				Now the Eleven Disciples		David Hurd
				Christ unser Herr zum Jordan kam, *Cantata 7*		J S Bach
				Additional Music		
■				All Glory Be to God on High	BFAS	J S Bach
	inst			All Glory Be to God on High		Johann Crüger
■				Credo		Multiple
■				Gloria		Multiple
			SATB, inst	God As Ribbon of Light		Libby Larsen
				I Arise Today		Libby Larsen
■				O Bread of Life from Heaven	BFAS	J S Bach
■				O Trinity, Most Blessed Light	AFC 1	C Kenneth Turner
■				We All Believe in One True God	BFAS	J S Bach
	■			Quoniam tu solus sanctus, *Mass in B Minor*		J S Bach
	■			Sanctis fortis, *Dream of Gerontius*		Edward Elgar
				Cantatas/Major Works		
				7: Christ unser Herr zum Jordan kam		J S Bach
				129: Gelobt sei der Herr, mein Gott		J S Bach
				The Creation		Franz Joseph Haydn

Entrance	Sequence	Offertory	Communion	Postcommunion		H82	WLP	LEVAS II	VF	MHSO	CG descant	Inst descant
		■			All glory be to God on high [S]	421						
■					Ancient of Days, who sittest throned in glory [S]	363						
■					Come, thou almighty King [S]	365						■
			■		Glory to God [S]					117		
■					God, beyond all human praises [S]		745					
■					God the sculptor of the mountains [S]		746,747			130		
■					Holy Father, great Creator [S]	368						■
■					Holy God, we praise thy Name [S]	366						
■			■		Holy, holy, holy! Lord God Almighty! [S]	362					■	■
■					How wondrous great, how glorious bright [S]	369						■
■					I bind unto myself today [S]	370						
			■		In the night, in the day [S]					116		
			■		Laus Trinitati / O praise be to you Holy Trinity [S]				105			
■					O God, we praise thee, and confess [S]	364						
			■		O threefold God of tender unity [S]		743					
			■		O Trinity of blessed light [S]	29,30	744				■	
■					Oh Lord, how perfect is your name [P]			57				
■					Round the Lord in glory seated [S]	367						
■					Sing praise to our Creator [S]	295						
					Genesis 1:1-2:4a							
■					All creatures of our God and King	400					■	
■					All things bright and beautiful	405			111,112			
■					Creator of all time and space				102			
		■			God of the sparrow God of the whale					129		
			■		He's got the whole world in his hand			217				
■					I sing the almighty power of God	398					0	
■					Immortal, invisible, God only wise	423						■
■					Let all things now living				107			
		■			Many and great, O God, are thy works	385				128		
■					Most High, omnipotent, good Lord	406,407						
					Most Holy God, the Lord of heaven	31,32					■	
■		■			O all ye works of God now come	428	884					
					O blest Creator, source of light (1-4)	27,28						
■					Queremos cantar / We sing a new song				113			
■					The spacious firmament on high	409						
■					The stars declare his glory	431						
■					Thou, whose almighty word	371					■	
		■			We are a part of all creation					131		
					2 Corinthians 13:11-13							
		■			Gracious Spirit, give your servants		782				0	
		■			Loving Creator, grant to your children					115		
		■			Praise to God, praise to God					132		
					Matthew 28:16-20							
■			■		Alleluia! sing to Jesus!	460,461						■
			■		If you love me, truly love me					83		
				■	Lord, you give the great commission	528	780				0	
				■	We are all one in mission		778				■	

0 Same tune, but not text [S] Seasonal [C] Collect [P] Psalm [GR] Gospel-related [SC] Semi-continuous

Anthem	Solo	Handbells	Voicing		Collection	Composer
PROPER 1 = SIXTH SUNDAY AFTER THE EPIPHANY						
PROPER 2 = SEVENTH SUNDAY AFTER THE EPIPHANY						
PROPER 3 = EIGHTH SUNDAY AFTER THE EPIPHANY						
				Genesis 6:9-22, 7:24; 8:14-19 SC Track		
			TBB	Sailorman Noah, *Four Folksongs and Spirituals*		David Johnson
				Psalm 46 SC Track		
				Ein feste Burg	BFAS	J S Bach
				God Is Now Our Sure Defense		Hugo Distler
			SSAATTBB	God Is Our Hope and Strength		Simon Preston
				God Is Our Refuge		Jan Bender
				God Is Our Refuge and Strength		W A Mozart
				In Ecclesiis		Giovanni Gabrieli
				O Salutaris Hostia		Multiple
				Psalm 46		David Cherwien
						John Ferguson
						Heinrich Schütz
				The Lord of Hosts Is With Us		Dudley Buck
			Unison	There Is a River		Benedetto Marcello
						Robert J Powell
				Timor et tremor		Multiple
				Why Do the Nations, *Messiah*		G F Handel
				Deuteronomy 11:18-21, 26-28 GR Track		
				Psalm 31: 1-5, 19-24 GR Track		
			SATTB	In manus tuas		Thomas Tallis
				In te, Domine		Josquin des Prez
						Heinrich Schütz
			SATTB	In te speravi		G P Palestrina
				In Thee O Lord		Thomas Weelkes
			Unison	In Thee O Lord Do I Put My Trust		Jan Bender
				In Thee, O Lord, Have I Trusted	CON	G F Handel
			Alto	In deine Hände befehl..., *Cantata 106*		J S Bach
				Romans 1:16-17; 3:22b-28 [29-31]		
				O Lord, Increase My Faith		Henry Loosemore
				Salvation Unto Us Has Come	BFAS	J S Bach
				Matthew 7:21-29		
				Christ Is Made the Sure Foundation		Dale Wood
				God Is a Rock		Robert Shaw/Alice Parker
			SA	Hosanna! Me Build a House		West Indian Folk Tune, arr Peek
				Tu es Petrus		Maurice Duruflé
						Gabriel Fauré
						G P Palestrina
						Charles-Marie Widor
				Cantatas/Major Works		
				45: Es ist dir gesagt, Mensch, was gut ist [Helm]		J S Bach

						H82	WLP	LEVAS II	VF	MHSO	CG descant	Inst descant
Entrance	Sequence	Offertory	Communion	Postcommunion								

PROPER 1 = SIXTH SUNDAY AFTER THE EPIPHANY

PROPER 2 = SEVENTH SUNDAY AFTER THE EPIPHANY

PROPER 3 = EIGHTH SUNDAY AFTER THE EPIPHANY

						H82	WLP	LEVAS II	VF	MHSO	CG descant	Inst descant
					A mighty fortress is our God [P 46]	687,688						
					Genesis 6:9-22; 7:24; 8:14-19 SC Track							
▪					Eternal Father, strong to save	608						▪
			▪		It rained on the earth forty days, forty nights (1,3-4)					97		
▪					Lord Jesus, think on me	641	798					
				▪	When the storms of life are raging			200				
					Deuteronomy 11:18-21,26-28 GR Track							
▪					Help us, O Lord, to learn	628						
▪					Lord, be thy word my rule	626						
			▪		O God, unseen yet ever near	332						
					Romans 1:16-17;3:22b-28(,29-31)							
▪					Amazing grace! how sweet the sound	671		181				▪
▪					Come, thou fount of every blessing	686		111			▪	▪
▪					Hail, thou once despised Jesus	495						
▪					O praise ye the Lord (1-2,4)	432						
					Matthew 7:21-29							
	▪				Before the Lord's eternal throne	391						▪
▪					Blessed Jesus, at thy word	440						
		▪	▪		Glorious things of thee are spoken	522,523						▪
			▪		If thou but trust in God to guide thee	635						
				▪	Lord, dismiss us with thy blessing	344						▪

▪ Same tune, but not text   [S] Seasonal   [C] Collect   [P] Psalm   [GR] Gospel-related   [SC] Semi-continuous

Anthem	Solo	Handbells	Voicing		Collection	Composer
				Genesis 12:1-9 SC Track		
			SSA	God's Promise		Samuel Adler
				Magnificat		Multiple
				Rock-a-My-Soul		arr Howard Roberts
				Psalm 33:1-12 SC Track		
				A Choral Flourish		Ralph Vaughan Williams
			2 pt	All Who Are Just		Couperin, arr Proulx
			SATB, 4 brass	Blessed Is the Nation		Donald Busarow
				Exsultate justi		Multiple
				Laudate Dominum in sanctis ejus		Multiple
			2 pt	Of the Kindness of the Lord		Richard Proulx
				Rejoice in the Lord		William Mathias
						Everett Titcomb
						Thomas Weelkes
				Hosea 5:15-6:6 GR Track		
			SA	Drop Down Ye Heavens	OXEA	Heathcote Statham
				Psalm 50:7-15 GR Track		
				Romans 4:13-25		
				Magnificat		Multiple
				O Lord, Increase My Faith		Henry Loosemoore
				Matthew 9:9-13, 18-26		
				Draw Us in the Spirit's Tether		Harold Friedell
				O Lord, Increase My Faith		Henry Loosemoore
				St. Matthew's Day		Alec Wyton
				Ach wie flüchtig, ach wie nightig, *Cantata 26*		J S Bach
				Courage, My Heart, *Rejoice Now My Spirit*		Georg Böhm
			Alto, Tenor, Bass	O Ewigkeit, du Donnerwort II *Cantata 60*		J S Bach
				Additional Music		
				There Is A Balm		arr William Dawson
				Precious Lord, Take My Hand		Thomas Dorsey
				There Is A Balm		Spiritual, Various
				Cantatas/Major Works		
				2: Ach Gott, vom Himmel sieh darein		J S Bach

Entrance	Sequence	Offertory	Communion	Postcommunion		H82	WLP	LEVAS II	VF	MHSO	CG descant	Inst descant
					Genesis 12:1-9 SC Track							
				■	O God of Bethel, by whose hand	709					■	■
■					The God of Abraham praise	401					■	■
			■		We are on our way to the promised land					96		
					Hosea 5:15-6:6 GR Track							
	■				The Second Song of Isaiah	S217-S222						
					Romans 4:13-18							
	■				Praise our great and gracious Lord	393						
					Matthew 9:9-13,18-26							
				■	A father came to Jesus				23			
	■				By all your saints still striving (2: St. Matthew)	231,232					■	
	■				From miles around the sick ones came		774					
		■			He sat to watch o'er customs paid	281						
				■	Heal me, hands of Jesus		773					
				■	Heal me, Lord				91			
			■		Hope of the world, thou Christ of great compassion	472						
	■				In your mercy, Lord, you called me	706						
			■		O Christ, the healer, we have come		772					
		■			O for a thousand tongues to sing	493						■
				■	O Jesus Christ, may grateful hymns be rising	590						
			■		There is a balm in Gilead	676	203					
			■		There was Jesus by the water				20			
		■			Thine arm, O Lord, in days of old	567					■	
			■		What does it mean to follow Jesus?					89		
	■				Will you come and follow me		757					
		■			You laid aside your rightful reputation		734					

Anthem	Solo	Handbells	Voicing		Collection	Composer
				Genesis 18:1-15, 21:1-7 SC Track		
▨				Laudate pueri		Multiple
▨				Magnificat		Multiple
				Psalm 116:1, 10-17 SC Track		
▨				Crediti - I Have Believed		Antonio Vivaldi
▨				My Tribute (To God Be the Glory)		Andrae Crouch
				Exodus 19:2-8a GR Track		
▨	▨			On Eagle's Wings		Michael Joncas
▨				The Lord Gave the Word, *Messiah*		G F Handel
				Psalm 100 GR Track		
▨			SAB	All from the Sun's Uprise	OXEA	Philip Tomblins
▨				All People That on Earth Do Dwell	AFC 1	Thomas Tallis
▨			Unison	Cry Out with Joy		Christopher Walker
▨				Jauchzet dem Herren		Heinrich Schütz
▨				Jubilate Deo		Multiple
▨				O Be Joyful		Multiple
▨				Psalm 100		Multiple
▨				The Old Hundredth Psalm Tune		Ralph Vaughan Williams
				Romans 5:1-8		
▨				God So Loved the World		Jan Bender
▨						Bob Chilcott
▨						Katherine K Davis
▨						Hugo Distler
▨						Orlando Gibbons
▨						John Goss
▨			Unison or 2 pt			John Horman
▨			SA			Joel Martinson
▨			SSATBB			Michael Praetorius
▨						Heinrich Schütz
▨						John Stainer
▨			SAB, instr			G P Telemann
▨						Melchoir Vulpius
▨						David Ashley White
	▨			Salvation Unto Us Has Come	BFAS	J S Bach
▨				Wondrous Love		Various
				Matthew 9:35-10:8 9-23		
▨				Happy and Blest Are They, *St. Paul*		Felix Mendelssohn
▨				How Lovely Are the Messengers, *St. Paul*		Felix Mendelssohn
▨				Lord, Thou Alone Art God, *St. Paul*		Felix Mendelssohn
▨	▨			But the Lord Is Mindful of His Own, *St. Paul*		Felix Mendelssohn
▨				Jerusalem, Jerusalem, *St. Paul*		Felix Mendelssohn
				Additional Music		
▨				Draw Us in the Spirit's Tether		Harold Friedell
				Cantatas/Major Works		
				104: Du Hirte Israel, höre		J S Bach

						H82	WLP	LEVAS II	VF	MHSO	CG descant	Inst descant
■					Lord, whose love through humble service [C]	610						
					Genesis 18:1-15(21:1-7) SC Track							
			■		God it was who said to Abraham (1,5)					85		
			■		It rained on the earth forty days, forty nights (2-4)					97		
	■				Rejoice for women brave (1-2)				18			
		■			The God of Abraham praise	401					■	
					Exodus 19:2-8a GR Track							
■		■			All people that on earth do dwell [P 100]	377,378						■
■					Before the Lord's eternal throne [P 100]	391						
			■		You who dwell in the shelter of the Lord		810					
					Romans 5:1-8							
		■			Come down, O Love divine	516					■	
		■			Come, thou fount of every blessing	686	111				■	
■					Hail, thou once despised Jesus!	495						
■					O love of God, how strong and true	455,456					■	
					Matthew 9:35-10:8(,9-23)							
			■		Awake, thou Spirit of the watchmen	540						
			■		Come, labor on	541						■
	■				For the fruit of all creation	424						
	■				Hark! the voice of Jesus calling			126				
	■				Hope of the word, thou Christ of great compassion	472						
			■		Lord, you give the great commission	528	780				⊙	
			■		My God, thy table now is spread	321					■	
		■			The grain is ripe: the harvest comes!				33			
				■	Ye servants of God, your Master proclaim	535						

Anthem	Solo	Handbells	Voicing		Collection	Composer
				Genesis 21:8-21 SC Track		
■				As Panting Deer Desire the Waterbrooks		David Ashley White
■				Like As the Hart		Herbert Howells
■				Magnificat		Multiple
■				Sicut cervus		Multiple
				Psalm 86:1-10, 16-17 SC Track		
■				Be Merciful Unto Me O Lord		John Blow
			Unison	Bow Down Thine Ear, *Twelve Songs of Praise*		Samuel Adler
				Bow Down Thine Ear to Our Prayer, *Elijah*		Felix Mendelssohn
				Bow Down Thy Ear	OXCAB	Anton Arensky
						John Blow
						César Franck
						G F Handel
						Carl F Mueller
						G P Palestrina
				Comfort, O Lord, the Soul of Thy Servant	OXCAB	William Crotch
			SSA	Give Ear O Lord Unto My Prayer		Healey Willan
				I Praise Thee O Lord, *St. Paul*		F Mendelssohn
				O Salutaris Hostia		Multiple
				Psalm 86		Jean Berger
						Gustav Holst
			SA or Unison	Thou O Lord, Art Lord God Alone		Jean-Baptiste Lully, arr Crandell
				Jeremiah 20:7-13 GR Track		
■				He Trusted in God, *Messiah*		G F Handel
■				Improperium expectavit		Orlando di Lasso
■				Like As the Hart		Herbert Howells
■				O vos omnes		Multiple
	■			Behold and See, *Messiah*		G F Handel
	■			But Thou Didst Not Leave, *Messiah*		G F Handel
	■			He Was Despised, *Messiah*		G F Handel
				Psalm 69:8-11 [12-17] 18-20 GR Track		
■				Hide Not Thou Thy Face	TUD	Richard Farrant
■				Improperium expectavit		Orlando di Lasso
■				Let Not Those Who Hope in You…		Robert Lind
■				Save Me, O God		John Blow
	■			Psalm 142, *Cycle of Holy Songs*		Ned Rorem
				Romans 6:1b-11		
■				Christ Being Raised from the Dead		John Blow
						Eric Thiman
			SSA			Healey Willan
				Christ, Our Passover		Richard Dirksen
						Will C MacFarlane
						Robert J Powell
						Ralph Vaughan Williams
				Christus resurgens		Orlando di Lasso
						Lodovico Viadana
			SATB, str	Christ Rising Again		William Byrd
						Thomas Weelkes
				Since By Man Came Death	SEW	Thomas Pavlechko
				The Risen Christ		T Tertius Noble
				There Is a Balm in Gilead		arr. William Dawson
	■		Alto	Vergügte Ruh, beliebte Seelenlust, *Cantata 170*		J S Bach
				Matthew 10:24-39		
■				Crux fidelis		Multiple
				Cantatas/Major Works		
				114: Ach, lieben Christen, seid getrost		J S Bach
				170: Vergügte Ruh', beliebte Seelenlust		J S Bach

						H82	WLP	LEVAS II	VF	MHSO	CG descant	Inst descant
					Praise to the living God! [C]	372					O	
					Genesis 21:8-21 SC Track							
		▪			You shall cross the barren desert		811					
					Jeremiah 20:7-13 GR Track							
▪					I love thy kingdom, Lord	524						
▪					Surely it is God who saves me	678,679						
					Romans 6:1b-11							
▪					All who believe and are baptized	298						
		▪			Alleluia, alleluia! Give thanks to the risen Lord!	178						▪
	▪				God's Paschal Lamb is sacrificed for us		880				O	
	▪				We know that Christ is raised and dies no more	296					O	
					Matthew 10:24-39							
			▪		Christ for the world we sing!	537						▪
			▪		Day by day	654				33		
			▪		He who would valiant be	564,565						
					I can hear my Savior calling			144				
					I have decided to follow Jesus			136				
					If when you give the best of your service			190				
					O Jesus, I have promised	655					▪	
	▪				Praise the Lord through every nation	484,485						
	▪				Spread, O spread, thou mighty word	530						
					Take up your cross, the Savior said	675						▪
	▪				They cast their nets in Galilee	661						
				▪	Will you come and follow me		757					

Anthem	Solo	Handbells	Voicing		Collection	Composer
				Collect		
				Christ Is Made the Sure Foundation		Dale Wood
				The Best of Rooms		Randall Thompson
				Tu es Petrus		Maurice Duruflé
						Gabriel Fauré
						G P Palestrina
						Charles-Marie Widor
				Genesis 22:1-14 SC Track		
				Abraham and Isaac		Benjamin Britten
				Little Lamb		David Cherwien
				The Lamb		John Tavener
				Psalm 13 SC Track		
				Hide Not Thou Thy Face	TUD	Richard Farrant
				How Long Wilt Thou Forget Me		Austin Lovelace
						Ned Rorem
				Illumina occulos meos		Orlando di Lasso
				Like As the Hart		Herbert Howells
			SS	Lord My Hope Is in Thee		Heinrich Schütz
				The 13th Psalm		Jean Berger
			SSA			Johannes Brahms
						Robert J Powell
						Heinrich Schütz
				Jeremiah 28:5-9 GR Track		
				Dona nobis pacem, *Mass in B Minor*, BWV232		J S Bach
				Peace Be Unto You		Knut Nystedt
				Peace, Perfect Peace		Libby Larsen
				Peace Be Unto You	LIFT	Franz Schubert
				Psalm 89:1-4, 15-18 GR Track		
				Dixit Dominus		Multiple
			2 pt	I Will Sing of Thy Mercies		Felix Mendelssohn
						Gerald Near
				Misericordias Domini		Multiple
				My Song Shall Be Always of the Loving-Kindness…		Gerald Near
				Thou Art the Glory…, *Chandos Anthem No 7*		G F Handel
				Your Love O Lord Forever Will I Sing		Peter Hallock
				Blessed Is the People…, *Chandos Anthem No 4*		G F Handel
				Romans 6:12-23		
				But Thanks Be to God, *Messiah*		G F Handel
				Christ Rising Again		William Byrd
			SAB	I Know That My Redeemer Lives		Drummond Wolff
				Salvation Unto Us Has Come	BFAS	J S Bach
				Since by Man Came Death, *Messiah*		G F Handel
				Since By Man Came Death	SEW	Thomas Pavlechko
			Soprano	I Know That My Redeemer Liveth, *Messiah*		G F Handel
			Alto, Tenor	O Death, Where Is thy Sting? *Messiah*		G F Handel
				Matthew 10:40-42		
				How Lovely Are the Messengers, *St. Paul*		Felix Mendelssohn
				In This House		Richard Smallwood
				Cantatas/Major Works		
				111: Was mein Gott will, das g'scheh allzeit		J S Bach

Entrance	Sequence	Offertory	Communion	Postcommunion		H82	WLP	LEVAS II	VF	MHSO	CG descant	Inst descant
■					Christ is made the sure foundation [C]	518					■	
					The Church's one foundation [C]	525					■	
					Genesis 22:1-18　SC Track							
	■				O sorrow deep! (2-4)	173						
■		■			The God of Abraham praise	401					■	
					Jeremiah 28:5-9　GR Track							
	■				Blessed be the God of Israel	444						
	■				Blessed be the God of Israel		889					
	■				O day of God draw nigh	600,601						
			■		O God of every nation	607						■
			■		Savior, again to thy dear Name we raise	345					■	
					Romans 6:12-23							
■					Creator of the stars of night (1-4,6)	60						
	■				Crown him with many crowns	494					■	
		■			Here, O my Lord, I see thee face to face	318						
■					Lord Jesus, think on me	641	798					
■					Now that the daylight fills the sky	3,4						
			■		Wilt thou forgive that sin, where I begun	140,141						
					Matthew 10:40-42							
	■				Gracious Spirit, give your servants		782				⊙	
			■		Lord, speak to me that I may speak				98			
			■		No saint on earth lives life to self alone		776					
			■		We are all one in mission		778				■	
				■	Where cross the crowded ways of life	609						

Anthem	Solo	Handbells	Voicing		Collection	Composer
				Genesis 24:34-38; 42-49, 58-67 SC Track		
				Psalm 45:11-18 SC Track		
X				Affrentur regi virgines		Anton Bruckner
X			SSATB	Constitues eos principes		Samuel Wesley
X				My Heart Is Inditing, *Coronation Anthem No 4*		G F Handel
X				O God My King	AFC 1	John Amner
				Song of Solomon 2:8-13 alt SC Track		
X				My Beloved Spake		Patrick Hadley
X				Nigra sum		Multiple
				Zechariah 9:9-12 GR Track		
X				Be Joyful, O Daughter of Zion		Everett Titcomb
X				Lift Up Your Heads	16th	John Amner
X				Lift Up Your Heads, *Messiah*		G F Handel
X				Lift Up Your Heads		William Mathias
X				My Heart Is Inditing, *Coronation Anthem No 4*		G F Handel
X			SA or TB	Rejoice Greatly		Healey Willan
	X		Soprano	Rejoice Greatly, *Messiah*		G F Handel
				Psalm 145:8-15 GR Track		
X				Hallelujah, *Messiah*		G F Handel
X				O God My King	AFC 1	John Amner
				Romans 7:15-25a		
X				Ich elender Mensch..., *Cantata 48*		J S Bach
				Matthew 11:16-19, 25-30		
X				Come Unto Me, Unison		Healey Willan
X				His Yoke Is Easy, *Messiah*		G F Handel
X				His Yoke Is Easy (Born to Die)		Glenn Burleigh
X				Lord of the Dance		arr John Ferguson
						David Willcocks
X				Tollite jugum meum		G P Palestrina
X			SATTB	Venite ad me omnes		Orlando di Lasso
X				What Boundless Love		Alfred V Fedak
	X			A Song of Trust		Franz Schubert
	X			Bye and Bye		Spiritual, arr Boatner
	X		Sop or Alto	He Shall Feed /Come Unto Him, *Messiah*		G F Handel
				Additional Music		
X			Unison, desc	A Prayer of St. Richard of Chichester	OXEA	L J White
				Cantatas/Major Works		
				113: Herr Jesu Christ, du höchstes Gut		J S Bach

Entrance	Sequence	Offertory	Communion	Postcommunion		H82	WLP	LEVAS II	VF	MHSO	CG descant	Inst descant
■				■	Love divine, all loves excelling [C]	657					■	
					Genesis 24:34-38,42-49.58-67 SC Track							
	■				Come away to the skies [canticle]	213						
	■				Lo, the winter's past [canticle]				145			
	■				O perfect Love, all human thought transcending				140			
					Zechariah 9:9-12 GR Track							
■					God my King, thy might confessing [P 145]	414					■	
■					Hail to the Lord's Anointed	616						
		■		■	Jesus shall reign, where'er the sun	544					■	
■					We will extol you, ever-blessed Lord [P145]	404						
					Romans 7:15-25a							
■					Awake, my soul, and with the sun	11						
		■			Hope of the world, thou Christ of great compassion	472						
			■		Just as I am, without one plea	693		137	82,83,84			■
					Matthew 11:16-19,25-30							
■					Blest be the King whose coming	74						
	■				Can we by searching find out God	476						
	■				Christ the worker	611						
	■				"Come to me, ye who are hard oppressed"			156				
			■		Father, we thank thee who hast planted	302,303						
				■	Go forth for God; go to the world in peace	347						
	■				How sweet the Name of Jesus sounds	644						
	■				I heard the voice of Jesus say	692						
	■				Lord of all hopefulness, Lord of all joy	482			131			■
			■		O Bread of life for sinners broken	342						
	■				Softly and tenderly Jesus is calling			101				
		■			Take my yoke upon you				127			
		■			Those who labor for the Lord				76			

Anthem	Solo	Handbells	Voicing		Collection	Composer
				Genesis 25:19-34 SC Track		
				Psalm 119:105-112 SC Track		
▓				A Canticle of Light		Richard Purvis
				Teach Me, O Lord, the Way of Thy Statutes		Thomas Attwood
				Thy Word Is a Lantern		Robert J Powell
						Henry Purcell
						Leo Sowerby
▓				**Isaiah 55:10-13 GR Track**		
				For Ye Shall Go Out with Joy		Emma Lou Diemer
				Seek the Lord		René Clausen
						Knut Nystedt
				This Is Our God		Paul Christiansen
				Ye Shall Go Out with Joy		Jean Berger
				You Shall Go Out with Joy		Carl Schalk
				Psalm 65:[1-8] 9-14 GR Track		
		▓	Unison, instr	God's Joyful Harvest		Robert J Powell
				Thou, Oh God, Art Praised in Sion		Malcolm Boyle
					AFC 4	Ian Hare
				Thou Visitest the Earth	OXCAB	Maurice Greene
	▓		Alto	Du Herr, du krönst, *Cantata 187*		J S Bach
				Romans 8:1-11		
▓				Behold the Lamb of God, *Messiah*		G F Handel
				But Thanks Be to God, *Messiah*		G F Handel
				Ev'ry Time I Feel the Spirit		Moses Hogan
				God So Loved the World		Bob Chilcott
						Hugo Distler
						Orlando Gibbons
						John Goss
						Heinrich Schütz
						John Stainer
▓				Salvation Unto Us Has Come	BFAS	J S Bach
	▓			Jesu meine Freude, BWV 227 (motet)		J S Bach
▓				Behold the Son of God	LIFT	W A Mozart
▓			Alto and Tenor	Then Shall be Brought/O Death, Where…, *Messiah*		G F Handel
				Matthew 13:1-9, 18-23		
▓				The Best of Rooms		Randall Thompson
				Cantatas/Major Works		
				18: Gleichwie der Regen und Schnee…		J S Bach
				68: Also hat Gott die Welt geliebt		J S Bach

	Entrance	Sequence	Offertory	Communion	Postcommunion		H82	WLP	LEVAS II	VF	MHSO	CG descant	Inst descant
						Genesis 25:19-34 SC Track							
		▓				Lamp of our feet, whereby we trace [P 119]	627						
		▓				O Christ, the Word Incarnate [P 119]	632						
						Isaiah 55:10-13 GR Track							
		▓				Surely it is God who saves me	678,679						
						Romans 8:1-11							
			▓			Eternal Spirit of the living Christ	698						
			▓			O Spirit of Life, O Spirit of God	505						
			▓			Spirit of the living God, fall fresh on me			115				
						Matthew 13:1-9,18-23							
		▓				Almighty God, your word is cast	588,589						
	▓					Blessed Jesus, at thy word	440						
		▓				Father, we thank thee who hast planted	302,303						
		▓	▓			Gentile or Jew, servant or free			151				
	▓			▓		God is working his purpose out	534						▓
			▓			Lord, make us servants of your peace	593						
			▓			Spread, O spread, thou mighty word	530						

Anthem	Solo	Handbells	Voicing		Collection	Composer
				Collect		
				Almighty God, the Fountain of All Wisdom	AFC 1	Ernest Farrar
						Thomas Weelkes
				Genesis 28:10-19a SC Track		
			Unison	As Jacob with Travel Was Weary One Day		Jack Noble White
				Locus iste		Multiple
				Surely the Lord Is in This House		Robert J Powell
				The Gate of Heaven		Randall Thompson
				The House of God		Joseph Clokey
				The Spirit of the Lord Is Here		Donnie McClurklin
				Truly the Lord Is In This Place		Peter Hurford
				We Are Climbing Jacob's Ladder		Spiritual, Various
				Psalm 139:1-11, 22-23 SC Track		
				If I Take the Wings of Morning		Amanda Husberg
				Thou Knowest, Lord, the Secrets...		Henry Purcell
				Thou Wilt Keep Him in Perfect Peace	OXCAB	Samuel Wesley
				Search Me, O God	LIFT	Antonín Dvorak
				Wisdom of Solomon 12:13, 16-19 GR Track		
				Isaiah 44:6-8 alt GR Track		
				Psalm 86:11-17 GR Track		
				For God Alone My Soul in Silence Waits		Peter Hallock
				I Praise Thee O Lord, *St. Paul*		Felix Mendelssohn
				O Salutaris Hostia		Multiple
				O For A Closer Walk with God	AFC 1	C V Stanford
				Psalm 86		Jean Berger
						Gustav Holst
				Teach Me, O Lord, the Way of Thy Statutes		Thomas Attwood
			SSA	Teach Me Thine Ways		Alan Hovhaness
				Teach Me Thy Way O Lord		John Blow
				Romans 8:12-25		
				As Many As Are Led By the Spirit		David McK Williams
				Matthew 13:24-30, 36-43		
				E'en So, Lord Jesus, Quickly Come		Paul Manz
				I Looked and Behold a White Cloud		Healey Willan
				Then Shall the Righteous Shine Forth, *Elijah*		Felix Mendelssohn
			Bass	He is Like a Refiner's Fire, *Messiah*		G F Handel
				Then Shall the Righteous Shine Forth, *Elijah*		Felix Mendelssohn
				Cantatas/Major Works		
				98: Was Gott tut, das ist wohlgetan		J S Bach

						H82	WLP	LEVAS II	VF	MHSO	CG descant	Inst descant
Genesis 28:10-19a SC Track												
		▓			As Jacob with travel was weary one day	453						
				▓	From my birth, from my birth [P 139]					126		
			▓		Lord, thou has searched me and dost know [P 139]	702						
				▓	We are climbing Jacob's ladder			220				
Wisdom 12:13,16-19 GR Track												
				▓	Eternal light, shine in my heart	465,466						▓
▓					Immortal, invisible, God only wise	423						▓
	▓				My God, how wonderful thou art	643						
▓					O day of God, draw nigh	600,601						
▓					The Lord will come and not be slow	462						
Isaiah 44:6-8 GR Track												
	▓				Come, thou almighty King	365						
▓					Praise to the living God	372					o	
▓					To God with gladness sing	399						
Romans 8:12-25												
	▓				All my hope on God is founded	665					▓	
▓					Christ is the world's true Light	542						
			▓		Come with us, O blessed Jesus	336						
▓					Creator of the stars of night	60						
Matthew 13:24-30,36-43												
	▓				Almighty God, your word is cast	588,589						
		▓			Come, labor on	541						▓
	▓				Come, ye thankful people, come (2-4)	290						
			▓		Father, we thank thee who hast planted	302,303						
	▓				For the fruit of all creation	424						
			▓		Gentile or Jew, servant or free			151				
	▓				God the sculptor of the mountains		746,747			130		

Anthem	Solo	Handbells	Voicing		Collection	Composer
				Genesis 29:15-28 SC Track		
				Psalm 105:1-11, 45b SC Track		
●				Confitemini Domino		Multiple
●				To God Be the Glory		arr M Roger Holland
				Psalm 128 alt SC Track		
●				Blessed Are They		Leo Sowerby
	●		Baritone	Happy Are You		Jane Marshall
●				How Blest Are They		Richard Proulx
				1 Kings 3:5-12 GR Track		
	●			What Though I Trace, *Solomon*		G F Handel
				Psalm 119:129-136 GR Track		
●				Gloria in Excelsis, *All Night Vigil*		Sergei Rachmaninoff
●				O For a Closer Walk with God	AFC 1	C V Stanford
●				O That I Love Your Law O Lord		J William Greene
●				Teach Me, O Lord, the Way of Thy Statutes		Thomas Attwood
●				Your Word Went Forth		Sally Ann Morris
				Romans 8:26-39		
●				All Things		Theron Kirk
●			Unison	God Works for Good		Jane Marshall
●				If God Be For Us		Carl F Mueller
●				Ist Gott für uns?		Heinrich Schütz
●				The Spirit Also Helpeth Us		J S Bach
●				Those Who Love the Lord		Theron Kirk
●				Wer will uns scheiden - Who shall separate us		Heinrich Schütz
	●			Was Gott tut, das ist wohlgetan, *Cantata 99*		J S Bach
	●			Das neugeborne Kindelein, BuxWV 13, st. 3		Dietrich Buxtehude
●				Der Geist hilft unsrer..., BWV 226 (motet)		J S Bach
	●			As the Wings of Doves, *Three Odes of Solomon*		Alan Hovhaness
	●			If God Be For Us, *Messiah*		G F Handel
	●			Who Shall Separate Us, *Letters from St. Paul*		Daniel Pinkham
				Matthew 13:31-33, 44-52		
●				Jesu, meine Freude	BFAS	J S Bach
●				Song of the Mustard Seed		Hal Hopson
				Cantatas/Major Works		
				71: Gott ist mein König		J S Bach

Entrance	Sequence	Offertory	Communion	Postcommunion		H82	WLP	LEVAS II	VF	MHSO	CG descant	Inst descant
				■	If thou but trust in God to guide thee [C]	635						
					Genesis 29:15-28 SC Track							
■		■			Not here for high and holy things	9						■
					1 Kings 3:5-12 GR Track							
	■				Be thou my vision, O Lord of my heart	488						■
			■		Eternal light, shine in my heart	465,466						
		■			Even when young, I prayed for wisdom's grace		906					
■					God, you have given us power to sound	584						
			■		Open your ears, O faithful people	536						
					Romans 8:26-39							
	■				Children of the heavenly father			213				
		■			Eternal Spirit of the living Christ	698						
■					God moves in a mysterious way	677						
■					God of grace and God of glory	594,595					■	
				■	Jesus lives! thy terrors now	194,195						
	■				Like the murmur of the dove's song	513						
				■	Spread, O spread, thou mighty word	530						
		■			The Christ who died but rose again	447						
					Matthew 13:31-33,44-52							
			■		In the bulb there is a flower					86		
		■			Seek ye first the kingdom of God	711						■
	■				The Lord will come and not be slow	462						
				■	"Thy kingdom come!" on bended knee	615						■
				■	Your kingdom come, O Lord					27		

■ Same tune, but not text   [S] Seasonal   [C] Collect   [P] Psalm   [GR] Gospel-related   [SC] Semi-continuous

Anthem	Solo	Handbells	Voicing		Collection	Composer
				Genesis 32:22-31 SC Track		
■				Come O Thou Traveler Unknown		Erik Routley
■				Wrestling Jacob		Malcolm Williamson
				Psalm 17:1-7, 16 SC Track		
■				Even Me		arr Nolan Williams
■			2 pt	Give Ear Unto Me		Benedetto Marcello
■				Lord, Thou Knowest		Andreas Hammerschmidt
■				O Lord, Attend My Cry		Jan P Sweelinck
■			Unison	Psalm 17		Jane Marshall
■				Thou Knowest, Lord, the Secrets of...		Thomas Morley
■						Henry Purcell
				Isaiah 55:1-5 GR Track		
■				Ho! Everyone That Thirsteth		Betty Carr Pulkingham
■				O Come Everyone That Thirsteth, *Elijah*		Felix Mendelssohn
■				Sicut cervus		Multiple
■				Sitientes, venite ad aquas		Tomás Luis de Victoria
	■		Quartet	Ho, Everyone Who Thirsts, *Elijah*		Felix Mendelssohn
				Psalm 145:8-9, 14-21 GR Track		
■				Every Eye Waiteth Upon Thee		Heinrich Schütz
■				O God My King	AFC 1	John Amner
■				Oculi Omnium		Charles Wood
■				Prope est Dominus	CHES	Jacob Regnart
■				The Eyes of All Wait Upon Thee		Jean Berger
■						William Harris
■			Unison			Richard Proulx
■				The Lord Is Good to All		Jean Berger
				Romans 9:1-5		
				Matthew 14:13-21		
■				How the Grandeur of Creation		Craig Phillips
■				O sacrum convivium		Multiple
■				Panis angelicus		Multiple
	■			Panis angelicus		César Franck
				Thine O Father, Thine Is…, *Fall of Jerusalem*	LIFT	Martin Blumner
				Additional Music		
	■			Love Bade Me Welcome, *Five Mystical Songs*		Ralph Vaughan Williams
				Cantatas/Major Works		
				177: Ich ruf zu dir, Herr Jesu Christ		J S Bach

Entrance	Sequence	Offertory	Communion	Postcommunion		H82	WLP	LEVAS II	VF	MHSO	CG descant	Inst descant
					Genesis 32:22-31 SC Track							
		▓			Come, O thou Traveler unknown	638,639						
			▓		With awe approach the mysteries		759					
					Isaiah 55:1-5 GR Track							
	▓				God, my King, thy might confessing [P 145]	414					▓	
▓					Surely it is God who saves me	678,679						
		▓			The eyes of all wait upon you, O Lord [P145]		820					
	▓				We will extol you, ever-blessed Lord [P 145]	404						
					Romans 9:1-5							
	▓				Lord, for ever at thy side	670						
▓			▓		O God of Bethel, by whose hand	709					▓	
▓					Open your ears, O faithful people	536						
					Matthew 14:13-21							
	▓				All who hunger gather gladly		761		87	52		
		▓			Bread of life, hope of the world					48		
			▓		Bread of the world, in mercy broken	301						
			▓		Break thou the bread of life			146	73			
			▓		Hope of the world, thou Christ of great compassion	472						
▓			▓		I come with joy to meet my Lord	304					▓	
			▓		Let us talents and tongues employ				79	50		
			▓		My God, thy table now is spread	321					▓	
			▓		O Food to pilgrims given	308,309						
			▓		O Wheat, whose crushing was for bread		760		74			
▓					We the Lord's people, heart and voice uniting	51					▓	

Anthem	Solo	Handbells	Voicing		Collection	Composer
				Genesis 37:1-4, 12-28 SC Track		
			TTB	Little Boy Joseph, *Four Folksongs & Spirituals*		David Johnson
				Psalm 105:1-6, 16-22, 45b SC Track		
				Confitemini Domino		Multiple
				O Give Thanks Unto the Lord		Jean Berger
			SAB			William Croft
						Michael Haydn
						Felix Mendelssohn
						Everett Titcomb
			ATTB			Thomas Tomkins
				Sing Unto Him with Psalms		Hans Leo Hassler
				Thanks Be to Yahweh		Heinrich Schütz
			Unison	We Will Sing for Joy		Domenico Scarlatti
				1 Kings 19:9-18 GR Track		
				Dear Lord and Father of Mankind		Charles H H Parry
				O Salutaris Hostia		Multiple
				It Is Enough, *Elijah*		Felix Mendelssohn
				Jerusalem, Jerusalem, *St. Paul*		Felix Mendelssohn
				Liebster Herr Jesu, *Five Spiritual Songs*		J S Bach
				Psalm 85:8-13 GR Track		
			SA	Drop Down Ye Heavens	OXEA	Heathcote Statham
				Mercy and Truth Are Met		Ned Rorem
				Romans 10:5-15		
				How Lovely Are the Messengers, *St. Paul*		Felix Mendelssohn
				If Thou Shalt Confess with Thy Mouth		C V Stanford
				Lovely Appear, *The Redemption*		Charles Gounod
				Their Sound Is Gone Out, *Messiah*		G F Handel
			Alto	How Beautiful are the Feet, *Messiah*		G F Handel
				Matthew 14:22-33		
			TTBB, fl	How Can I Keep From Singing		arr Bradley Ellingboe
				O Lord, Increase My Faith		Henry Loosemoore
				Peace, Be Still		arr Nolan Williams
				How Can I Keep From Singing		Various
				Additional Music		
				Fürchte dich nicht, BWV 228 (motet)		J S Bach

	Entrance	Sequence	Offertory	Communion	Postcommunion		H82	WLP	LEVAS II	VF	MHSO	CG descant	Inst descant
Genesis 37:1-4,12-28 SC Track													
From deepest woe I cry to thee		■					151						
Out of the depths I call		■					666						
1 Kings 19:9-18 GR Track													
Dear Lord and Father of mankind				■			652,653						■
Praise the Spirit in creation				■			506,507					■	
The Lord will come and not be slow [P85]	■						462						
Romans 10:5-15													
At the Name of Jesus		■					435			135			■
In Christ there is no East or West	■						529		62			■	
Matthew 14:22-33													
Commit thou all that grieves thee			■				669						■
Eternal Father, strong to save		■					608						
Give praise and glory unto God				■			375						
How firm a foundation, ye saints of the Lord		■					636,637						
I sought the Lord, and afterward I knew				■			689						
I was sinking deep in sin			■						198				
Jesus, Lover of my soul							699		79			■	
Lead us, heavenly Father, lead us				■			559						
O all ye works of God, now come		■					428	884					
O God, our help in ages past	■			■			680						
O worship the King, all glorious above	■						388						
Precious Lord, take my hand				■				800	106				
When the storms of life are raging									200				

Anthem	Solo	Handbells	Voicing		Collection	Composer
				Genesis 45:1-15 SC Track		
				The Eyes of All Wait Upon Thee		Jean Berger
				Psalm 133 SC Track		
			SATTBB	Behold How Good a Thing		William Byrd
				Behold, How Good, and How Pleasant		Daniel Pinkham
				Behold, How Good and Joyful	AFC 1	John Clarke-Whitfeld
			SATBB	Behold, How Good and Pleasant It Is		Hans Leo Hassler
						Ned Rorem
				Chichester Psalms		Leonard Bernstein
				Psalm 133		Ronald Arnatt
			TTBB			Leo Sowerby
				Isaiah 56:1, 6-8 GR Track		
				Coventry Antiphon		Herbert Howells
				I Rejoiced When I Heard Them Say		Richard Proulx
				I Was Glad		Ronald Arnatt
						William Boyce
						Frank Ferko
			2 pt			Peter Hallock
			SSATTB			Charles H H Parry
						Henry Purcell
						Leo Sowerby
				Jubilate Deo Ps 100		Multiple
				Laetatus sum		Marc-Antonio Charpentier
						Michael Haydn
						Claudio Monteverdi
				Locus iste		J. Aiblinger
						Anton Bruckner
			SATB, divisi	Look Toward the East		Thomas Pavlechko
				Look Toward the East		Richard Webster
				The Gate of Heaven		Randall Thompson
				Psalm 67 GR Track		
				Deus, misereatur nostri		Heinrich Schütz
			2 pt treble	God Be Merciful		Paul Bouman
						Alan Hovhaness
						Christopher Tye
			SSA			Healey Willan
			Unison, 2 vln	Let the People Praise Thee O God		Andreas Hammerschmidt
			SA			Robert J Powell
						Martin Shaw
			SS			Healey Willan
				Let All the Peoples Praise You O God		William Mathias
				O God Be Merciful	16th	Christopher Tye
				O Let the Nations Be Glad		Randall Thompson
				Psalm 67		Jane Marshall
						David Ashley White
				Thou, O God, Art Praised in Sion		Malcolm Boyle
				Romans 11:1-2a, 29-32		
				One Bread, One Body		John Foley
				Matthew 15:[10-20] 21-28		
				Great Is Thy Faithfulness		arr Don Hart
				It Is Not Fair		Jan Bender
				Lauda Sion		Multiple
				Liebster Jesu, hör mein Flehen		Johann Michael Bach
				O Jesu, fili David		Josquin des Prez
				The Daughter		Alice Parker
				Cantatas/Major Works		
				51: Jauchzet Gott in allen Landen!		J S Bach

						H82	WLP	LEVAS II	VF	MHSO	CG descant	Inst descant
					Genesis 45:1-15 SC Track							
	▨				God moves in a mysterious way	677						
					Isaiah 56:1,6-8 GR Track							
▨		▨			From all that dwell below the skies	380						▨
▨					God of mercy, God of grace [P 67]	538						▨
▨					How wondrous and great thy works, God of praise!	532,533						
			▨		My God, thy table now is spread	321					▨	▨
		▨			Only-begotten, Word of God eternal	360,361						▨
▨					We the Lord's people, heart and voice uniting	51					▨	
					Romans 11:1-2a,29-32							
	▨				In your mercy, Lord, you called me	706						
▨					Praise, my soul, the King of heaven	410						
		▨			Sing praise to God who reigns above	408					▨	
			▨		There's a wideness in God's mercy	469,470						▨
					Matthew 15:10-20							
	▨				In boldness look to God for help				94			▨
			▨		O Spirit of the living God	531						
			▨		O Zion, haste, thy mission high fulfilling	539						▨
			▨		Pass me not, O gentle Savior			139				
				▨	Thou, whose almighty word	371					▨	

Anthem	Solo	Handbells	Voicing		Collection	Composer
				Exodus 1:8-2:10 SC Track		
				And the Children of Israel..., *Israel in Egypt*		G F Handel
				Now There Arose..., *Israel in Egypt*		G F Handel
				Psalm 124 SC Track		
				A Song of Battle		C V Stanford
				Psalm 124		Alice Parker/Robert Shaw
			TTBB			Leo Sowerby
			Soprano	If God Be For Us, *Messiah*		G F Handel
				Isaiah 51:1-6 GR Track		
				Comfort Ye, My People		George Thalben-Ball
			SSA	Lift Thine Eyes, *Elijah*		Felix Mendelssohn
				O Comfort Now My People	SEW	Thomas Pavlechko
				Psalm 138 GR Track		
			Unison	A Joyous Psalm		Eugene Butler
				Confitebor tibi, *Solemn Vespers*		W A Mozart
				Locus iste		Multiple
			SAB	O Give Thanks Unto the Lord		John Wood
				Psalm 138		Knut Nystedt
						J P Sweelinck
				Give God the Glory		Heinrich Schütz
				Romans 12:1-8		
			SATB opt inst	We Are One In Christ		Richard Hillert
				One Bread, One Body		John Foley
				Matthew 16:13-20		
				Hymn to St. Peter		Benjamin Britten
				I Go to the Rock		George Briggs, Dottie Rambo/arr L Larson
				True Anointed One		David Ashley White
			SAB	Tu es pastor		Claudio Monteverdi
				Tu es Petrus		Maurice Duruflé
						Gabriel Fauré
					CHES	Hans Leo Hassler
			SAB			Cristobal Morales
						G P Palestrina
						Charles-Marie Widor
				Jesus, Redeemer		Anton Bruckner
				Cantatas/Major Works		
				92: Ich hab in Gottes Herz und Sinn		J S Bach
				Israel in Egypt		G F Handel

Title	H82	WLP	LEVAS II	VF	MHSO	CG descant	Inst descant
Come now, O Prince of Peace [C]		795			82		
I come with joy to meet my Lord [C]	304						
Our Father, by whose Name [C]	587						
Praise the Lord, rise up rejoicing [C]	334						
Put forth, O God, thy Spirit's might [C]	521						
Thou, who at thy first Eucharist didst pray [C]	315						
Unidos/Together [C]		796					
Exodus 1:8-2:10 SC Track							
O wind that blows on the river of reeds				19			
Isaiah 51:1-6 GR Track							
God it was who said to Abraham (1,5)					85		
The desert shall rejoice		722					
The God of Abraham praise	401						
To God with gladness sing	399						
Romans 12:1-8							
God is Love, and where true love is	576,577						
Gracious Spirit, give your servants		782				0	
Holy Spirit, font of light	228						
Like the murmur of the dove's song	513						
Lord, you give the great commission	528	780				0	
Muchos resplandores / Many are the lightbeams		794					
O Holy Spirit, by whose breath	501,502						
Take my life, and let it be	707			132,133			
Ubi caritas et amor		831					
Where charity and love prevail	581						
Matthew 16:13-20							
From God Christ's deity came forth	443						
Glorious things of thee are spoken	522,523						
The Church's one foundation	525						
You are the Christ, O Lord	254						

Same tune, but not text [S] Seasonal [C] Collect [P] Psalm [GR] Gospel-related [SC] Semi-continuous

133

Anthem	Solo	Handbells	Voicing		Collection	Composer
				Exodus 3:1-15 SC Track		
				De profundis		Multiple
				Out of the Depths		Jacques Charpentier
				Out of the Deep, *Requiem*		John Rutter
				Psalm 130		Multiple
				Psalm 105:1-6, 23-26, 45c SC Track		
				Confitemini Domino		Multiple
				O Give Thanks Unto the Lord		Jean Berger
			SAB			William Croft
						Michael Haydn
						Felix Mendelssohn
						Everett Titcomb
			ATTB			Thomas Tomkins
				Sing Unto Him with Psalms		Hans Leo Hassler
				Thanks Be to Yahweh		Heinrich Schütz
			Unison	We Will Sing for Joy		Domenico Scarlatti
				Jeremiah 15:15-21 GR Track		
				Lord, Thou Knowest		Andreas Hammerschmidt
				Lord, Thou Knowest All My Desire		John Blow
				Thou Knowest, Lord, the Secrets		Thomas Morley
						Henry Purcell
				Psalm 26:1-8 GR Track		
	SS			Examine Me, O Lord		William Boyce, arr W Shaw
	SSA			Judica me, Domine		Orlando di Lasso
				Locus iste		Multiple
				Lord, I Have Loved Thy Habitations		Gerald Near
			SAATB	O Lord, I Have Loved		Thomas Tomkins
				O Lord, My God to Thee		Jacques Arcadelt
				Romans 12:9-21		
				Be Ye Followers of God		Leo Sowerby
				My Dear Brethren, *Three Sacred Concertos*		Hugo Distler
				Matthew 16:21-28		
				Be Ye Followers of God		Leo Sowerby
				Dear Lord and Father of Mankind		Charles H H Parry
				Lord of the Dance		arr John Ferguson
					100 CFC	arr David Willcocks
			2 pt	Qui vult venire		Orlando di Lasso
				Jesus nahm zu sich die Zwölfe, *Cantata 22*		J S Bach
				I Follow Thee Gladly, *St. John Passion*		J S Bach
			Bass	Jesus Calling Then the Twelve, *Cantata 22*		J S Bach
			Alto	My Savior, Take Thou Me, *Cantata 22*		J S Bach
			Bass	Ich will den Kreuzstab gerne..., *Cantata 56*		J S Bach
				Additional Music		
				O God, My Heart Is Ready		Simon Lindley
				Cantatas/Major Works		
				Israel in Egypt		G F Handel

	Entrance	Sequence	Offertory	Communion	Postcommunion		H82	WLP	LEVAS II	VF	MHSO	CG descant	Inst descant
					■	Lord, dismiss us with thy blessing [C]	344						■
		■				We plow the fields, and scatter [C]	291						
						Exodus 3:1-15 SC Track							
			■			What wondrous love is this	439						■
	■					The God of Abraham praise	401					■	
			■			We sing of God, the mighty source	386,387						
						When from bondage we are summoned		753,754				■	
	■					When Israel was in Egypt's land	648		228				
						Jeremiah 15:15-21 GR Track							
	■		■			If thou but trust in God to guide thee	635						
						Lord, speak to me that I may speak				98			
						Surely it is God who saves me	678,679						
						Romans 12:9-21							
						Cuando el pobre nada tiene / When the poor one who has nothing		802					
						God is Love, and where true love is	576,577						
		■				Gracious Spirit, give your servants		782				0	
	■					Holy Spirit, font of light	228						
				■		Like the murmur of the dove's song	513						
					■	Lord, whose love through humble service	610						
						O Holy Spirit, by whose breath	501,502						
						Put peace into each other's hands		790					
				■		Take my life, and let it be	707			132,133			
	■				■	The church of Christ in every age		779				■	
			■			Ubi caritas et amor		831					
						Where charity and love prevail	581						
						Where true charity and love dwell	606						
						Matthew 16:21-28							
			■			Day by day	654				33		
						I can hear my Savior calling			144				
						I have decided to follow Jesus			136				
	■					New every morning is the love	10						
						Praise the Lord through every nation	484,485						
						Take up your cross, the Savior said	675						■
				■		Will you come and follow me		757					
						You laid aside your rightful reputation		734					

Anthem	Solo	Handbells	Voicing		Collection	Composer
				Exodus 12:1-14 SC Track		
				O Mary, Don't You Weep		Carl MaultsBy
				Psalm 149 SC Track		
				A Processional Psalm for a Festive Occasion		Peter Hallock
				An Anthem of Praise	CON 2	Antonin Dvorak
				Cantate Domino		Multiple
				Hallelujah! Sing to the Lord a New Song		Bruce Neswick
			Unison	O Sing to the Lord		Donald Pearson
				O Sing Unto the Lord a New Song		Multiple
			SSAATTBB	Singet dem Herrn ein neues Lied, BWV 225		J S Bach
				Ezekiel 33:7-11 GR Track		
				Turn Back, O Man		Gustav Holst
				Psalm 119:33-40 GR Track		
				Gloria in excelsis, *All Night Vigil*		Sergei Rachmaninoff
				O For a Closer Walk with God	AFC 1	C V Stanford
			Unison	O Turn Away Mine Eyes		William Boyce
				Oh How I Love Your Law, O Lord!		J William Greene
				Teach Me, O Lord, the Way of Thy Statutes		Thomas Attwood
					TUD	William Byrd
						David Hurd
			Unis/2 pt, perc			Knut Nystedt
				Romans 13:8-14		
				Rejoice, O Jerusalem, Behold, Thy King Cometh		Healey Willan
				The Night Is Far Spent		Knut Nystedt
				Ubi caritas		Maurice Duruflé
				Hemmet den Eifer, verbannet die Rache		G P Telemann
				Now It Is High Time..., *Letters from St. Paul*		Daniel Pinkham
				Matthew 18:15-20		
				Draw Us in the Spirit's Tether		Harold Friedell
				Lord, I Want to Be a Christian		Brazeal Wayne Dennard
				Ubi caritas		Maurice Duruflé
				Cantatas/Major Works		
				170:Vergnügte Ruh', beliebte Seelenlust		J S Bach
				Israel in Egypt		G F Handel
			SSAATTBB	Singet dem Herrn ein neues..., BWV 225 (motet)		J S Bach

Entrance	Sequence	Offertory	Communion	Postcommunion		H82	WLP	LEVAS II	VF	MHSO	CG descant	Inst descant
					Exodus 12:1-14　SC Track							
		■			At the Lamb's high feast we sing	174						■
			■		The Lamb's high banquet called to share	202						
					Ezekiel 33:7-11　GR Track							
	■				Come, ye disconsolate			147				
■					From deepest woe I cry to thee	151						
■					Lord Jesus, think on me, and purge away my sin	641	798					
■					'Tis the gift to be simple	554						
					Romans 13:8-14							
■					Awake, my soul, and with the sun	11						
					Awake, my soul, stretch every nerve	546					■	
					Awake, thou Spirit of the watchmen	540						
			■		Circle the table, hands now extend				85			
					Eternal Ruler of the ceaseless round	617						
		■			For the fruit of all creation	424						
		■			Jesu, Jesu, fill us with your love	602	74					
					Matthew 18:15-20							
■					All creatures of our God and King	400					■	
	■				Blessed Jesus, at thy word	440						
■					Christ is made the sure foundation	518					■	
			■		Come now, O Prince of peace		795			82		
	■				Father, we thank thee who hast planted	302,303						
			■		"Forgive our sins as we forgive"	674					■	
■					God is love, and where true love is	576,577					■	
■					Joyful, joyful, we adore thee	376					■	
			■		Lord, make us servants of your peace	593					■	
				■	Singing songs of expectation	527					■	
			■		Unidos/Together		796					
			■		We are all one in mission		778				■	
					We gather at your table, Lord				89			
			■		Where charity and love prevail	581						
			■		Where true charity and love dwell	606						

Anthem	Solo	Handbells	Voicing		Collection	Composer
				Exodus 14:19-31 SC Track		
				Wade in the Water		Spiritual, Various
				God Hath Led His People On	LIFT	Felix Mendelssohn
				Psalm 114 SC Track		
			SATB/SATB	In exitu Israel - When Israel Came		Samuel Wesley
						Antonio Vivaldi
				Psalm 114		Zoltan Kodaly
				When Israel Came Out of Egypt		William Byrd
				When Israel Went Out of Egypt		Hans Leo Hassler
				Exodus 15:1b-11, 20-21 (canticle alt) SC Track		
				A Song of Exultation		Samuel Adler
				And I Will Exalt Him		G F Handel
				Cantemus Domino		Felice Anerio
			Unison	I Will Sing to the Lord		Alec Wyton
				Sing to the Lord		Carolyn Jennings
				Sing Ye to the Lord		Edward Bairstow
			SSA	The Song of Miriam		Nathaniel Dett
			2 pt	The Song of Moses		Betty Carr Pulkingham
				Who Is Like Unto Thee		Jean Berger
				Israel in Egypt		G F Handel
				Genesis 50:15-21 GR Track		
				The Eyes of All Wait Upon Thee		Jean Berger
				Psalm 103:[1-7] 8-13 GR Track		
				Benedic anima mea	CHES	Claudin de Sermisy
				Bless the Lord		Ippolitov-Ivanov
				Bless the Lord, O My soul		Austin Lovelace
			2 pt or 3 pt	Like As a Father		Luigi Cherubini
				Lord for Thy Tender Mercy's Sake	TUD	Richard Farrant
				Not Only Unto Him/Bless Now..., *St. Paul*		Felix Mendelssohn
				Praise the Lord, O My Soul		Thomas Tomkins
				Romans 14:1-12		
				At the Name of Jesus		Ralph Vaughan Williams
				Christus factus est		Multiple
				Glory and Worship, *Coronation Anthem No 3*		G F Handel
				Let Justice and..., *Coronation Anthem No 2*		G F Handel
			SSATB	No Man Liveth Unto Himself		Heinrich Schütz
				Pues si vivimos - While We Are Living		Alice Parker
				Matthew 18:21-35		
				Ubi caritas		Maurice Duruflé
			3 pt	You Wicked Servant		Jan Bender
				Mach dich, mein Geist, bereit, *Cantata 115*		J S Bach
			Tenor	Ich armer Mensch, ich..., *Cantata 55*		J S Bach
			Sop, Alto, Bass	Was soll ich aus dir machen..., *Cantata 89*		J S Bach
				Additional Music		
				Go Down, Moses		arr Hall Johnson
				Cantatas/Major Works		
				69a: Lobe den Herrn, meine Seele		J S Bach

						H82	WLP	LEVAS II	VF	MHSO	CG descant	Inst descant
Exodus 14:19-31 SC Track												
Come, sing the joy of Miriam									121			
Guide me, O thou great Jehovah						690						
Praise our great and gracious Lord						393						
Sing now with joy unto the Lord						425						
We give thanks unto you, O God of might										98		
When Israel was in Egypt's land						648		228				
Wisdom freed a holy people							905		155			
Genesis 50:15-21 GR Track												
All my hope on God is founded						665						
Bless the Lord, my soul [P 103]							825					
God moves in a mysterious way						677						
In the bulb there is a flower										86		
O bless the Lord, my soul [P 103]						411						
Praise, my soul, the King of Heaven [P 103]						410						
Praise to the Lord, the Almighty, the King of creation [P 103]						390						
Romans 14:1-12												
Creator of the stars of night						60						
Crown him with many crowns						494						
Jesus, our mighty Lord, our strength in sadness						478						
No saint on earth lives life to self alone							776					
Matthew 18:21-25												
All creatures of our God and King						400						
Come now, O Prince of peace							795			82		
"Forgive our sins as we forgive"						674						
Go forth for God, go to the world in peace						347						
God is Love, and where true love is						576,577						
Joyful, joyful, we adore thee						376						
Lord, make us servants of your peace						593						
Most High, omnipotent, good Lord						406,407						
Praise the Lord, rise up rejoicing						334						
Where charity and love prevail						581						
Where true charity and love dwell						606						

The leftmost columns are: Entrance, Sequence, Offertory, Communion, Postcommunion

Same tune, but not text   [S] Seasonal   [C] Collect   [P] Psalm   [GR] Gospel-related   [SC] Semi-continuous

Anthem	Solo	Handbells	Voicing		Collection	Composer
				Exodus 16:2-15 SC Track		
				Lauda Sion		Multiple
				The Eyes of All Wait Upon Thee		Jean Berger
				God Hath Led His People On	LIFT	Felix Mendelssohn
				Panis angelicus		César Franck
				Psalm 105:1-6, 37-45 SC Track		
				Confitemini Domino		Multiple
				O Give Thanks Unto the Lord		Jean Berger
			SAB			William Croft
						Michael Haydn
						Felix Mendelssohn
						Everett Titcomb
			ATTB			Thomas Tomkins
				Panis angelicus		Multiple
				Sing Unto Him With Psalms		Hans Leo Hassler
				Thanks Be to Yahweh		Heinrich Schütz
				The Eyes of All Wait Upon Thee		Jean Berger
			Unison	We Will Sing for Joy		Domenico Scarlatti
				Jonah 3:10-4:11 GR Track		
				Psalm 145:1-8 GR Track		
				All Thy Works Shall Praise Thee		William Mathias
			2 pt	Der Herr ist Gross		Heinrich Schütz
				Great Is the Lord		Jean Berger
				I Will Extol Thee		Jean Berger
			SATB, Unison			Wilbur Held
						Jane Marshall
				I Will Extol You		Emma Lou Diemer
						Peter Hallock
				O God My King	AFC 1	John Amner
				O Lord I Will Praise Thee	OXEA	Gordon Jacob
				Every Day Will I Give Thanks	LIFT	G F Handel
				Philippians 1:21-30		
				Come, Sweetest Death	OXEA	J S Bach
				Jesus Christ the Apple Tree	100 CFC	Elizabeth Poston
				Steal Away		arr Dale Adelmann
						arr William Dawson
				The Apple Tree		K Lee Scott
				Bist du bei mir		J S Bach
				Come Sweetest Death	OXEA	J S Bach
				Five Spiritual Songs - *Geistlich Lieder*		J S Bach
				Consider Then, My Soul Unwary		
				Come, Celebrate This Morn		
				Dearest Lord Jesus		
				Come, Soothing Death		
				If Thou Art Near		
				Steal Away		Spiritual, Various
				Matthew 20:1-16		
				Simile est regnum	CHES	Cristobal Morales
				Nimm, was dein ist, und gehe hin, *Cantata 144*		J S Bach
				Steal Away		Various
			Soprano	Ich bin vergnügt mit meinem Glücke, *Cantata 84*		J S Bach
				Additional Music		
				Ain'a That Good News		arr William Dawson
						Spiritual, Various
				He Is the Rock		Michael Barrett
				Cantatas/Major Works		
				92: Ich hab in Gottes Herz und Sinn		J S Bach

						H82	WLP	LEVAS II	VF	MHSO	CG descant	Inst descant
Entrance	Sequence	Offertory	Communion	Postcommunion								

Exodus 16:2-15 SC Track

Title	H82	WLP	LEVAS II	VF	MHSO
All who hunger gather gladly		761		87	52
Glorious things of thee are spoken	522,523				
God be with you till we meet again		801			
Guide me, O thou great Jehovah	690				
How sweet the Name of Jesus sounds	644				
Lamp of our feet, whereby we trace	627				
Lord, enthroned in heavenly splendor	307				
O Food to pilgrims given	308,309				
Shepherd of souls, refresh and bless	343				

Jonah 3:10-4:11 GR Track

Title	H82
Give praise and glory unto God	375
God, my King, thy might confessing [P 145]	414
O bless the Lord, my soul	411
Praise, my soul, the King of heaven	410
We will extol you, ever-blessed Lord [P 145]	404

Philippians 1:21-30

Title	H82	WLP
Eternal Ruler of the ceaseless round	617	
For thy dear saints, O Lord	279	
God be in my head	694	
My God, accept my heart this day	697	
Singing songs of expectation	527	
We are all one in mission		778

Matthew 20:1-16

Title	H82	LEVAS II	VF	MHSO
Christ the worker	611			
Come, labor on	541			
For the bread which you have broken	340,341			
From glory to glory advancing, we praise thee, O Lord	326			
Jesus in the morning		76		
Lord of all hopefulness, Lord of all joy	482		131	
Not here for high and holy things	9			
O Jesus, I have promised	655			
O Master, let me walk with thee	659,660			
Rise up, ye saints of God	551			
Strengthen for service, Lord	312			
Those who labor for the Lord			76	

Same tune, but not text   [S] Seasonal   [C] Collect   [P] Psalm   [GR] Gospel-related   [SC] Semi-continuous

Anthem	Solo	Handbells	Voicing		Collection	Composer
				Exodus 17:1-7 SC Track		
				Wade in the Water		Spiritual, Various
				God Hath Led His People On	LIFT	Felix Mendelssohn
				Psalm 78:1-4, 12-16 SC Track		
			SATB/SATB	In exitu Israel - When Israel Came Out		Samuel Wesley
						Antonio Vivaldi
				When Israel Came Out of Egypt		William Byrd
				When Israel Went Out of Egypt		Hans Leo Hassler
				Ezekiel 18:1-4, 25-32 GR Track		
				Create in Me, O God		Johannes Brahms
				Cast Me Not Away…		
				Grant Unto Me the Joy of Thy Salvation		
				Create in Me		Carl F Mueller
				Lord, for Thy Tender Mercy's Sake	TUD	Richard Farrant
				Miserere mei, Deus		Multiple
				Turn Thy Face from My Sins	OXCAB	Thomas Attwood
				Psalm 25:1-9 GR Track		
				Call to Remembrance, O Lord	TUD	Richard Farrant
			SSAATTBB			John Hilton
				Leite mich in deiner Wahrheit…, *Cantata 150*		J S Bach
				Lord, Make Me to Know Thy Ways		William Byrd, arr Lovelace
				Nach dir, Herr, verlanget mich, *Cantata 150*		J S Bach
				Psalm 25		Harold Friedell
			Unison or 2 pt	Psalm for Advent		John Karl Hirten
				Show Me Thy Ways		Walter Pelz
			SAB	Show Me Your Ways		F J Haydn
				Teach Me O Lord		Thomas Attwood
						William Byrd
						David Hurd
			TB	To Thee, O Lord		Benedetto Marcello
					AFC 1	Sergei Rachmaninoff
				To Thee, O Lord, Have I Lifted Up My Soul		Gerald Near
				To You O Lord I Lift Up My Soul		Sam Batt Owens
				Universi, qui te exspectant		Michael Haydn
			SATB or 2 pt	Unto Thee I Lift Up My Soul		Franz Schubert
					LIFT	Peter Cornelius
				Philippians 2:1-13		
				Adoramus te, Christe		Multiple
				At the Name of Jesus		Ralph Vaughan Williams
				Christus factus est		Multiple
				Jesu, dulcis memoria		Multiple
			SAB	Jesus, Name of Wondrous Love		Everett Titcomb
				Let This Mind Be in You		Lee Hoiby
				Let Thy Hand Be…, *Coronation Anthem No 2*		G F Handel
				Non nobis, Domine		Multiple
				Praise to You Lord Jesus	CHAN	Heinrich Schütz
				Matthew 21:23-32		
				All Who Believe and Are Baptized	BFAS	J S Bach
				Let Justice and…, *Coronation Anthem No 2*		G F Handel
				Salvation Unto Us Has Come	BFAS	J S Bach
				Additional Music		
			SAT	Christ Did It All		Rodney Posey
				Cantatas/Major Works		
				87: Bisher habt ihr nichts gebeten		J S Bach

Entrance	Sequence	Offertory	Communion	Postcommunion		H82	WLP	LEVAS II	VF	MHSO	CG descant	Inst descant
					Exodus 17:1-7 SC Track							
■	■				Come, thou fount of every blessing	686		111			■	
■	■				Glorious things of thee are spoken	522,523					■	
■				■	Guide me, O thou great Jehovah	690						
			■		O Food to pilgrims given	309						
	■				O God, unseen yet ever near	332						
	■				Rock of ages, cleft for me	685						■
			■		Shepherd of souls, refresh and flesh	343					■	
	■				Surely it is God who saves me	678,679						
					Ezekiel 18:1-4,25-32 GR Track							
	■				Before thy throne, O God, we kneel	574,575						■
		■			'Tis the gift to be simple	554						
					Philippians 2:1-13							
■					All hail the power of Jesus' Name!	450,451					■	
	■				All praise to thee, for thou, O King divine	477						
	■				At the name of Jesus	435			135			
			■		Gracious Spirit, give your servants		782				0	
					Morning glory, starlit sky	585						
	■				O Spirit of the living God	531						
■	■				Sing, ye faithful, sing with gladness	492					■	
					The head that once was crowned with thorns	483						
	■				What wondrous love is this	439						■
		■			You laid aside your rightful reputation		734					
					Matthew 21:23-32							
			■		Deck thyself, my soul, with gladness	339						
				■	Lord, dismiss us with thy blessing	344						■
		■			Lord, we have come at your own invitation	348						
					O day of God, draw nigh	600,601						
				■	When we walk with the Lord			205				

Anthem	Solo	Handbells	Voicing		Collection	Composer
				Exodus 20:1-4, 7-9, 12-20 SC Track		
▪				Teach Me O Lord		Thomas Attwood
▪						William Byrd
▪						David Hurd
▪				The Holy Ten Commandments		F J Haydn
	▪			God Hath Led His People On	LIFT	Felix Mendelssohn
				Psalm 19 SC Track		
			SSATTB	Die Himmel erzahlen die Ehre Gottes		Heinrich Schütz
				Heaven and Earth..., *Twelve Songs of Praise*		Samuel Adler
				Let the Words of My Mouth		Henry Purcell
						K Lee Scott
						Everett Titcomb
				Psalm 19		Benedetto Marcello
						Richard Proulx
				The Heavens Are Telling	CON 1	Ludwig van Beethoven
				The Heavens Are Telling, *The Creation*		F J Haydn
				The Heavens Declare		William Billings
			TTBB			Thomas Tomkins
				The Heavens Declare God's..., *Samson*		G F Handel
				The Heavens Tell Out the Glory of God		Daniel Pinkham
				The Law of the Lord		William Mathias
				The Law of the Lord Is Perfect		Alec Wyton
				Their Sound Is Gone Out, *Messiah*		G F Handel
	▪			Die Himmel erzählen die Ehre..., *Cantata 76*		J S Bach
				Isaiah 5:1-7 GR Track		
▪	▪		SA	The Song of the Vineyard		Thomas Keesecker
▪				Vinea mea electa		Multiple
				Psalm 80:7-14 GR Track		
				Philippians 3:4b-14		
▪				Since by Man Came Death, *Messiah*		G F Handel
▪					SEW	Thomas Pavlechko
				Matthew 21:33-46		
▪				Built on a Rock the Church Doth Stand		arr. Knut Nystedt
				Christ Is Made the Sure Foundation		Dale Wood
				Christ Is Our Peace		Paul Nicholson
▪				Glory and Worship, *Coronation Anthem No 3*		G F Handel
				Jerusalem, Jerusalem, *St. Paul*		Felix Mendelssohn
				The Church's One Foundation		arr M Roger Holland
				Cantatas/Major Works		
				101: Nimm von uns, Herr, du treuer Gott		J S Bach

	Entrance	Sequence	Offertory	Communion	Postcommunion		H82	WLP	LEVAS II	VF	MHSO	CG descant	Inst descant
					■	Eternal Spirit of the living Christ [C]	698						
	■					Only-begotten, Word of God eternal [C]	360,361						
						Exodus 20:1-4,7-9,12-20 SC Track							
					■	Every time I feel the Spirit		751	114				
		■			■	Help us, O Lord, to learn	628						
					■	Most High, omnipotent, good Lord	406,407						
	■					Praise to the living God	372					o	
		■				The stars declare his glory [P 19]	431						
						Isaiah 5:1-7 GR Track							
						God the sculptor of the mountains		746,747			130		
			■			Open your ears, O faithful people	536						
						Philippians 3:4b-14							
		■				Awake, my soul, stretch every nerve	546					■	
		■				Fight the good fight with all thy might (1-2)	552,553						
			■			If the world from you withhold			197				
		■				I'm pressing on the upward way			165				
		■				Jesus, all my gladness	701						
	■					Lo! what a cloud of witnesses	545						
						Not far beyond the sea, nor high	422						
	■					We sing the praise of him who died	471						
					■	When from bondage we are summoned		753,754				■	
			■			When I survey the wondrous cross	474					■	■
						Matthew 21:33-46							
	■	■				Christ is made the sure foundation	518					■	
				■		Hail, thou once despised Jesus	495						■
				■		Lord Christ, when first thou cam'st to earth	598					■	
		■				My song is love unknown (1-2, 5)	458						
		■				O love, how deep, how broad, how high	448,449					■	
		■				The great Creator of the worlds	489						
			■			The head that once was crowned with thorns	483						
			■			Thou didst leave thy throne and thy kingly crown				126			

Anthem	Solo	Handbells	Voicing		Collection	Composer
				Exodus 32:1-14 SC Track		
				Ah, Thou Poor World	AFC 1	Johannes Brahms
				Confitemini Domino		Multiple
				Create in Me, O God		Johannes Brahms
				Cast Me Not Away From Thy…		
				Grant Unto Me the Joy of Thy Salvation		
				Create in Me		Carl F Mueller
				Lord for Thy Tender Mercies Sake		Richard Farrant
				Miserere mei, Deus		Multiple
				Turn Thy Face from My Sins	OXCAB	Thomas Attwood
				Consume Them All, Lord Sabaoth, *St. Paul*		Felix Mendelssohn
				God Hath Led His People On	LIFT	Felix Mendelssohn
				Psalm 106:1-6, 19-23 SC Track		
				Isaiah 25:1-9 GR Track		
				I Praise Thee, *St. Paul*		Felix Mendelssohn
				Today Hath Salvation Come, *All Night Vigil*		Sergei Rachmaninoff
				Psalm 23 GR Track		
				Brother James' Air		Gordon Jacob
				Flocks in Pastures Green Abiding	OXEA	J S Bach
				Lauda Sion		Multiple
			2 pt	My Shepherd Is Lord		Harrison Oxley
				Psalm 23		Multiple
						Ronald Arnatt
			SSAA			Martin How
						Thomas Matthews
						Walter Pelz
						Franz Schubert
				The Lord Is My Shepherd		Howard Goodall
					AFC 2	Maurice Greene
						C V Stanford
			2 pt canon			Gregg Smith
						Randall Thompson
					OXCAB	Samuel Wesley
				The Lord Is My Shepherd, *Requiem*		John Rutter
				The Lord My Shepherd		David Ashley White
				Yea Though I Wander		Georg Schumann
				Philippians 4:1-9		
				Rejoice in the Lord Always	16th	Anon
					OXCAB	Henry G Ley
						Henry Purcell
						Healey Willan
				But the Lord Is Mindful of His Own		Felix Mendelssohn
				O Rejoice in the…, *Three Sacred Concertos*		Hugo Distler
				Peace Be Unto You		Franz Schubert
				Rejoice in the Lord Always, *Letters from Paul*		Daniel Pinkham
				We Come Rejoicing		Carol Cymbala
				Matthew 22:1-14		
				I Sat Down Under His Shadow		Edward Bairstow
				O Sacred Communion	SEW	Larry Long
				O sacrum convivium		Multiple
				Schmücke dich, o liebe Seele, *Cantata 180*		J S Bach
				Jerusalem, Jerusalem, *St. Paul*		Felix Mendelssohn
			Soprano, Bass	Ich geh und suche mit Verlangen, *Cantata 49*		J S Bach
			S, A, T, B	Ach! Ich sehe, jetzt, da ich…, *Cantata 162*		J S Bach
				Cantatas/Major Works		
				Israel in Egypt		G F Handel

						H82	WLP	LEVAS II	VF	MHSO	CG descant	Inst descant
Exodus 32:1-14 SC Track												
					God the Omnipotent! King, who ordainest	569						
					O for a closer walk with God	683,684						
					Sing praise to God who reigns above	408					o	
Isaiah 25:1-9 GR Track												
					Glory, love, and praise and honor	300						
					My God, thy table now is spread	321						
					My Shepherd will supply my need [P 23]	664						
					The King of love my shepherd is [P 23]	645,646						
					The Lord is my shepherd [P 23]			104				
					The Lord my God my shepherd is [P 23]	663						
					The Lord, the Lord, the Lord is my shepherd [P 23]					102		
Philippians 4:1-9												
					Christ, who glory fills the skies	6,7						
					Holy Ghost, dispel our sadness	515						
					Jesus, all my gladness	701						
					Rejoice in the Lord always				162			
					Rejoice, the Lord is King	481						
					Rejoice, ye pure in heart	556,557						
					Savior, again to thy dear name we raise	345						
Matthew 22:1-14												
					As we gather at your Table		763				o	
					Come, my Way, my Truth, my Life	487						
					Deck thyself, my soul, with gladness	339						
					O Jesus, joy of loving hearts	649,650						
					The Lamb's high banquet called to share	202						
					This is the hour of banquet and of song	316,317						
					We gather at your table, Lord				89			
					We the Lord's people	51						

o Same tune, but not text   [S] Seasonal   [C] Collect   [P] Psalm   [GR] Gospel-related   [SC] Semi-continuous

Anthem	Solo	Handbells	Voicing		Collection	Composer
				Exodus 33:12-23 SC Track		
▨				Give God the Glory		J Hill
▨				Great and Glorious		F J Haydn
▨				The Lord Bless You and Keep You		Peter Lutkin
□						John Rutter
▨				**Psalm 99 SC Track**		
▨				Der Herr ist König		J Pachelbel
▨				Dominus regnavit		Peter Hallock
▨				Exalt Ye the Lord		Eric Thiman
▨				Great and Glorious		F J Haydn
▨				Te Deum		Multiple
▨				The Lord is King		David Ashley White
▨				**Isaiah 45:1-7 GR Track**		
▨				Great and Glorious		F J Haydn
▨				Te Deum		Multiple
▨				**Psalm 96:1-9, 10-13 GR Track**		
▨				Cantate Domino		Multiple
			SSAATB	Laetentur caeli	CHES	Jacob Handl
▨				O Sing Unto the Lord		Multiple
				1 Thessalonians 1:1-10		
				Matthew 22:15-22		
▨				Give Almes of Thy Goods		Christopher Tye
▨				Give God the Glory		J Hill
		▨		Wohl dem, der sich auf..., *Cantata 139*		J S Bach
▨	Soprano			Falsche Welt, dir trau ich nicht, *Cantata 52*		J S Bach
	S, A, T, B			Nur jedem das Seine, *Cantata 163*		J S Bach
				Additional Music		
▨				Rorate caeli (Isaiah 45:8)	CHES	Francisco Guerrero

Entrance	Sequence	Offertory	Communion	Postcommunion		H82	WLP	LEVAS II	VF	MHSO	CG descant	Inst descant
					Exodus 33:12-23 SC Track							
■		■			Holy, holy, holy! Lord God Almighty	362					■	
					Immortal, invisible, God only wise	423						■
		■	■		Rock of ages, cleft for me	685						■
					Isaiah 45:1-7 GR Track							
■		■			All people that on earth do dwell	377,378						■
■					Before the Lord's eternal throne	391						
■		■			Earth and all stars [P 96]	412						
■					Praise to the living God	372					o	■
■		■			Sing praise to God who reigns above	408					o	
					1 Thessalonians 1:1-10							
			■		I sought the Lord, and afterward I knew	689						
	■				In your mercy, Lord, you called me	706						
					Jesus, our mighty Lord	478						
			■		Lord, we have come at your own invitation	348						
			■		O for a closer walk with God	683,684						
					Matthew 22:15-22							
■			■		All my hope on God is founded	665					■	
	■				Father eternal, Ruler of creation	573						
■			■		God of grace and God of glory	594,595					■	
	■		■		Jesus shall reign, where'er the sun	544					■	
			■		Judge eternal, throned in splendor	596						
		■	■		O God of earth and altar	591						

Anthem	Solo	Handbells	Voicing		Collection	Composer
				Collect		
■				O Lord, Increase Our Faith		Henry Loosemoore
■				Thee We Adore		T Frederick Candlyn
				Deuteronomy 34:1-12 SC Track		
				Psalm 90:1-6, 13-17 SC Track		
■				Domine, refugium factus es nobis		Alessandro Scarlatti
■				Hymn of Praise		René Clausen
■				Lord, Thou Hast Been Our Dwelling Place		Ronald Arnatt
■						Frank Ferko
■						William Mathias
■			SATB/SATB	Lord, Thou Hast Been Our Refuge		Ralph Vaughan Williams
■						Edward Bairstow
■			brass quartet	O God Our Help in Ages Past		W Croft, arr Ferguson
■						Alan Hovhaness
■				O How Amiable		Ralph Vaughan Williams
■				O Lord, Thou Hast Been Our Dwelling Place		Carl Schalk
■				Thou, Lord, Our Refuge	OXCAB	Felix Mendelssohn
■				Turn Thee Again, O Lord	OXCAB	Thomas Attwood
				Leviticus 19:1-2, 15-18 GR Track		
■				Let Justice and…, *Coronation Anthem No 2*		G F Handel
■				The Ten Commandments		Jane Marshall
				Psalm 1 GR Track		
■	SA			Beatus vir		Orlando di Lasso
■						W A Mozart
■	SA			Blessed Is He Who Walks Not…		Heinrich Schütz
■	SAB			Blessed Is the Man		Archangelo Corelli
■						Jane Marshall
■				Blessed Is the Man, *All Night Vigil*		Sergei Rachmaninoff
■				Blest Is the Man		Hans Leo Hassler
■	SSA					Orlando di Lasso
■			Unison, ob, fl	Happy Is the Man Who Fears the Lord		Richard Proulx
■				O for a Closer Walk		C V Stanford
				1 Thessalonians 2:1-8		
■				Ubi caritas		Multiple
				Matthew 22:34-46		
■				God Is Love in *Playing Gospel Piano*		Carl MaultsBy
■				God Speaks Words of Love		Jane Marshall
■				If Ye Love Me		Daniel Pinkham
■						Thomas Tallis
■						Healey Willan
■						Philip Wilby
■		■		Herr Christ, der einge Gottessohn, *Cantata 96*		J S Bach
■				Give Me Your Hand	SOS	Spiritual, arr Boatner
		■	Alto	Gott soll allein mein Herze…, *Cantata 169*		J S Bach

						H82	WLP	LEVAS II	VF	MHSO	CG descant	Inst descant
Entrance	**Sequence**	**Offertory**	**Communion**	**Postcommunion**								
					Deuteronomy 34:1-12 SC Track							
▓		▓		▓	O God, our help in ages past [P 90]	680					▓	
▓		▓			Praise to the living God	372					o	
					Leviticus 19:1-2,15-18 GR Track							
		▓			Before thy throne, O God, we kneel	574,575						▓
					Father all-loving, who rulest in majesty	568						
▓					Give praise and glory unto God	375						▓
▓					Thy strong word did cleave the darkness	381						▓
					1 Thessalonians 2:1-8							
		▓			Brother, sister let me serve you				124	94		
▓					God of mercy, God of grace	538						
		▓			Lord, make us servants of your peace	593						
▓					O Spirit of the living God	531						
		▓			Take my life, and let it be	707			132,133			
					Matthew 22:34-46							
	▓				All hail the power of Jesus' Name!	450,451					▓	▓
			▓		Come with us, O blessed Jesus	336						
			▓		Jesu, Jesu, fill us with your love	602		74				
			▓		Jesus said: The first commandment is this		815					
		▓			Lord, whose love through humble service	610						
			▓		O Spirit of Life, O Spirit of God	505						
				▓	Rise up, ye saints of God	551					▓	
			▓		Where charity and love prevail	581						

Anthem	Solo	Handbells	Voicing		Collection	Composer
				Joshua 3:7-17 SC Track		
				Psalm 107:1-17, 33-37 SC Track		
				A Psalm of Thanksgiving		Randall Thompson
				Confitemini Domino		Multiple
				O Comfort Now My People	SEW	Thomas Pavlechko
				O Give Thanks to the Lord		Emma Lou Diemer
				The Love of the Lord		Joseph Gelineau
				Micah 3:5-12 GR Track		
				Fight the Good Fight		John Gardner
						Leo Sowerby
				Psalm 43 GR Track		
			SSA	Deus auribus nostris		Orlando di Lasso
			with TTB solos	Give Sentence with Me O God		Henry Purcell
				Hope in God		Jean Berger
				Judge Me, O God	OXCAB	Felix Mendelssohn
				Judica me, Deus		Heinrich Isaac
				O Send Out Thy Light		Milya Balakirev
						Charles Gounod
			2 pt			Maurice Greene
			SA	Oh Send Out Thy Light		Healey Willan
				Why Art Thou Cast Down, O My Soul?		Jean Berger
				Why Art Thou So Heavy, O My Soul?		Henry Loosemoore
				Why Art Thou Cast Down, My Soul?	LIFT	Felix Mendelssohn
				I Thessalonians 2:9-13		
				Ain'a That Good News		arr William Dawson
				Lo, Round the Throne		Henry Ley
				O Happy Souls		Alice Parker
				Matthew 23:1-12		
				At the Name of Jesus		Ralph Vaughan Williams
				Christus factus est		Multiple
				He That Is Down Need Fear No Fall		Philip Moore
			Unison			Ralph Vaughan Williams
				Let This Mind Be in You		Lee Hoiby
				Non nobis, Domine		Multiple
				Speak to Me in *K Franklin and Family*		Kirk Franklin
			Tenor	Ev'ry Valley, *Messiah*		G F Handel
				Cantatas/Major Works		
			Alto	169: Gott soll allein mein Herze haben		J S Bach

| | | | | | | H82 | WLP | LEVAS II | VF | MHSO | CG descant | Inst descant |
Entrance	Sequence	Offertory	Communion	Postcommunion								
					Awake, my soul, stretch every nerve [C]	546					■	
					Fight the good fight with all thy might [C]	552,553						
					Great is thy faithfulness [P 107]			189				
					Lo! what a cloud of witnesses [C]	545						
					Joshua 3:7-17 SC Track							
					Deep river, my home is over Jordan			8				
					Guide me, O thou great Jehovah	690					■	
					On Jordan's stormy banks			9				
					Micah 3:5-12 GR Track							
					Before thy throne, O God, we kneel	574,575						■
					O God of earth and altar	591						
					1 Thessalonians 2:9-13							
					Christ is the King! O friends upraise	614						
					From the dawning of creation		748					
					Lamp of our feet, whereby we trace	627						
					O Christ, the Word Incarnate	632						
					Matthew 23:1-12							
					All my hope on God is founded	665					■	
					Blest are the pure in heart	656						
					Brother, sister, let me serve you				124	94		
					Lord, for ever at thy side	670						
					O Jesus Christ, may grateful hymns be rising	590						
					Strengthen for service, Lord	312						
					Tell out, my soul, the greatness of the Lord	437,438					■	
					The church of Christ in every age		779					
					These three are the treasures to strive for and prize		803					

Anthem	Solo	Handbells	Voicing		Collection	Composer
				Joshua 24:1-3a, 14-25 SC Track		
				Jubilate Deo		Multiple
				O Be Joyful in the Lord		Multiple
				Psalm 100		Multiple
				Psalm 78:1-7 SC Track		
				Gloria in Excelsis, *All Night Vigil*		Sergei Rachmaninoff
				Teach Me, O Lord, the Way of Thy Statutes		Thomas Atwood
						William Byrd
						David Hurd
						Knut Nystedt
				Wisdom of Solomon 6:12-16 GR Track		
				Amos 5:18-24 (alt) GR Track		
				Lo! He Comes With Clouds Descending		David H Williams
				Timor et tremor		Multiple
				Thus Says the Lord, *Messiah*		G F Handel
				But Who May Abide, *Messiah*		G F Handel
				Wisdom of Solomon 6:17-20 (canticle - alt) GR Track		
				If Ye Love Me		Daniel Pinkham
						Thomas Tallis
						Philip Wilby
						Healey Willan
				Psalm 70 (alt) GR Track		
				Deus in adjutorum		J Pachelbel
			Unison	Hasten, O God, to Redeem Me		Heinrich Schütz
				Haste Thee, O God	AFC 1	Adrian Batten
				Psalm 70		David Ashley White
				The Seventieth Psalm		Ned Rorem
				Hasten, O Lord, to Redeem Me		Heinrich Schütz
				1 Thessalonians 4:13-18		
				If We Believe That Jesus Died	OXCAB	John Goss
				Du Friedefürst, Herr Jesu Christ, *Cantata 116*		J S Bach
				My Lord, What a Morning		Spiritual, Various
				The Trumpet Shall Sound, *Messiah*		G F Handel
				Tuba mirum, *Requiem*		Multiple
				Wachet auf		arr J S Bach
			Alto, Ten, Bass	Es reisset euch ein schrecklich..., *Cantata 90*		J S Bach
				Matthew 25:1-13		
				Audivi vocem de coelo		Thomas Tallis
				Dearest Lord Jesu	OXEA	J S Bach
				Keep Your Lamps		André Thomas
			3 pt	My Lord, What a Morning		arr Page
				Out of Your Sleep	100 CFC, CFC 2	Richard Rodney Bennett
				Sleepers, Wake!	AFC 1	Felix Mendelssohn
			SSATB, 2 vln	Therefore Watch That Ye Be Ready		Andreas Hammerschmidt
				Wachet auf		harm J S Bach
				Watchman, Tell Us of the Night		Alan Hovhaness
				Zion Hears the Watchman Singing	BFAS	harm J S Bach
				Wachet auf, ruft uns die..., *Cantata 140*		J S Bach
				My Lord, What a Morning		Spiritual, Various

Entrance	Sequence	Offertory	Communion	Postcommunion		H82	WLP	LEVAS II	VF	MHSO	CG descant	Inst descant
			■		O heavenly Word, eternal Light [C]	63,64						
					Joshua 24:1-3a,14-25 SC Track							
■		■			Guide me, O thou great Jehovah	690					■	
	■				O God of Bethel, by whose hand	709					■	
					Praise our great and gracious Lord	393						
					Wisdom 6:12-16 GR Track							
	■				Come and seek the ways of Wisdom				60			
					Even when young, I prayed for wisdom's grace		906					
					Amos 5:18-24 GR Track							
■					Before thy throne, O God, we kneel	574,575						■
■					Judge eternal, throned in splendor	596						
					Signs of ending all around us		721					■
	■				The Lord will come and not be slow	462						
					1 Thessalonians 4:13-18							
■					Jerusalem, my happy home	620					■	
		■			Jesus came, adored by angels	454						
	■				Jesus lives! Thy terrors now	194,195						
			■		Let all mortal flesh keep silence	324						
■					Lo, he comes with clouds descending	57,58					■	
■					Rejoice, the Lord is King!	481						
					Matthew 25:1-13							
				■	Lift up your heads, ye mighty gates	436						■
			■		Once he came in blessing	53						
			■		Rejoice, rejoice believers	68						
				■	"Sleepers, wake!" A voice astounds us	61,62						

Anthem	Solo	Handbells	Voicing		Collection	Composer
				Judges 4:1-7 SC Track		
▨				Lord, How Long Wilt Thou Be Angry		Henry Purcell
				Psalm 123 SC Track		
▨				Kyrie		Multiple
▨				Lift Thine Eyes, *Elijah* SSA (Ps. 121)		Felix Mendelssohn
▨				Oculi omnium		Charles Wood
▨				The Eyes of All Wait Upon Thee		Jean Berger
						William Harris
						Gerald Near
			Unison			Richard Proulx
				Zephaniah 1:7-12-18 GR Track		
▨				Awake the Trumpet's Lofty Sound, *Samson*		G F Handel
▨				O Salutaris Hostia		Multiple
▨				Tuba mirum, *Requiem*		Multiple
	▨		Alto	He Is Like a Refiner's Fire, (But who may abide) *Messiah*		G F Handel
			Bass	The Trumpet Shall Sound, *Messiah*		G F Handel
				Psalm 90:1-8, 9-11, 12 GR Track		
▨				Domine, refugium factus es nobis		Alessandro Scarlatti
▨				Hymn of Praise		René Clausen
▨				Lord, Thou Hast Been Our Dwelling Place		Ronald Arnatt
						Frank Ferko
						William Mathias
			SATB/SATB	Lord, Thou Hast Been Our Refuge		Ralph Vaughan Williams
						Edward Bairstow
			brass quartet	O God Our Help in Ages Past		William Croft, arr Ferguson
						Alan Hovhaness
				O How Amiable		Ralph Vaughan Williams
			2 pt	O Lord, My God, You Are My Refuge		J S Bach, arr Hopson
				O Lord, Thou Hast Been Our Dwelling Place		Carl Schalk
				Thou, Lord, Our Refuge	OXCAB	Felix Mendelssohn
				Turn Thee Again, O Lord	OXCAB	Thomas Attwood
▨			Tenor	Ach, Herr, lehre uns bedenken, *Cantata 106*		J S Bach
				Thessalonians 5:1-11		
▨				Be Ye Followers of God		Leo Sowerby
▨				Don't Let Him Catch You		Ashford & Simpson
▨				Out of Your Sleep	100 CFC, CFC 2	Richard Rodney Bennett
▨				Sleepers, Wake!	AFC 1	Felix Mendelssohn
				The Armor of God		John Ness Beck
			SSATB, 2 vln / cont	Therefore Watch That Ye Be Ready		Andreas Hammerschmidt
▨				Wachet auf		harm J Bach
▨				Watchman, Tell Us of the Night		Alan Hovhaness
▨				Zion Hears the Watchman Singing	BFAS	harm J S Bach
	▨			But of the Times and..., *Letters from St. Paul*		Daniel Pinkham
▨				My Lord, What a Morning		Spiritual, Various
				Matthew 25:14-30		
▨				Ecce sacerdos		Multiple
▨				Inherit the Kingdom		Lee Hoiby
			SA	Serve bone		Orlando di Lasso
				Additional Music		
▨				Glory and Worship		Henry Purcell
				Cantatas/Major Works		
				14: Wär Gott nicht mit uns diese Zeit		J S Bach
				140: Wachet auf, ruft uns die Stimme		J S Bach

Entrance	Sequence	Offertory	Communion	Postcommunion		H82	WLP	LEVAS II	VF	MHSO	CG descant	Inst descant
	■				Help us, O Lord, to learn [C]							
	■				Lord, be thy word my rule [C]							
■					O Christ, the Word Incarnate [C]	632						
			■		Word of God, come down on earth [C]	633						
					Judges 4:1-7 SC Track							
	■				Devorah, the prophet was a judge in Israel				17			
	■			■	Open your ears, O faithful people	536						
			■		With awe approach the mysteries		759					
					Zephaniah 1:7,12-18 GR Track							
■					Before thy throne, O God we kneel	574,575						■
■		■		■	O God, our help in ages past [P 90]	680					■	■
	■				Signs of ending all around us		721					■
	■				The Lord will come and not be slow	462						
					1 Thessalonians 5:1-11							
	■				Awake, O sleeper, rise from death	547						
	■				Eternal ruler of the ceaseless round	617						
	■				Hark! a thrilling voice is sounding	59						
			■		I want to walk as a child of the light	490						■
					Matthew 25:14-30							
			■		From glory to glory advancing, we praise thee, O Lord	326						
		■			Lord Christ, when first thou cam'st to earth	598					■	
		■			Not here for high and holy things	9						■
			■		O Jesus, I have promised	655					■	
			■		Once he came in blessing	53						
				■	Rise up, ye saints of God	551					■	
				■	Strengthen for service, Lord	312						

■ Same tune, but not text   [S] Seasonal   [C] Collect   [P] Psalm   [GR] Gospel-related   [SC] Semi-continuous

Anthem	Solo	Handbells	Voicing		Collection	Composer
				Ezekiel 34:11-16, 20-24 SC Track		
				See GR Track		
				Psalm 100 SC Track		
■			SAB	All from the Sun's Uprise	OXEA	Philip Tomblins
				All People That on Earth Do Dwell	AFC 1	Thomas Tallis
				Cry Out with Joy		Christopher Walker
				Jauchzet dem Herren		Heinrich Schütz
			SAB	Jubilate Deo		Agostino Agazzari
				Make a Joyful Noise		arr Don Hart
				O Be Joyful (Psalm 100)		Multiple
				Old Hundredth Psalm Tune		Ralph Vaughan Williams
				Ezekiel 34:11-16, 20-24 GR Track		
■				All We Like Sheep, *Messiah*		G F Handel
■				Kings Shall Be Thy…, *Coron. Anthem No 4*		G F Handel
				Lauda Sion		Multiple
				O quam gloriosum	CHES	Jacob Vaet
				Surrexit a mortuis		Charles-Marie Widor
				Surrexit pastor bonus		Multiple
■				These Are They Which Follow the Lamb	AFC 1	John Goss
	■		Sop or Alto	He Shall Feed His Flock, *Messiah*		G F Handel
				Psalm 95:1-7a GR Track		
■				Come Let Us Rejoice		John Amner
■				Come Let Us Sing to the Lord		Jack Noble White
■				My Heart is Inditing, *Coronation Anthem No 4*		G F Handel
■				O Come Let Us Sing Unto the Lord		Emma Lou Diemer
						Anthony Piccolo
						K Lee Scott
				O Come Let Us Worship, *All Night Vigil*		Sergei Rachmaninoff
				Sing to the Lord		Christopher Tye
			SAB			Johann Schein, arr Nelson
	■			O Come, Let Us Worship	LIFT	G F Handel
				Ephesians 1:15-23		
■				Adoramus te, Christe		Multiple
■				At the Name of Jesus		Ralph Vaughan Williams
■				Christus factus est		Multiple
■				Glory and Worship, *Coronation Anthem No 3*		G F Handel
■				Jesus! Name of Wondrous Love		Everett Titcomb
			SAB	Let Thy Hand be…, *Coronation Anthem No 2*		G F Handel
■				The King Shall Rejoice, *Coron. Anthem No 3*		G F Handel
				Matthew 25:31-46		
■				Ain'a That Good News		arr William Dawson
■				Give Almes of Thy Goods		Christopher Tye
■				Kings Shall Be Thy…, *Coron. Anthem No 4*		G F Handel
■				Let All the Angels of God, *Messiah*		G F Handel
■				Let Justice and Judgment, *Coron. Anthem No 2*		G F Handel
■				Lift Up Your Heads	16th	John Amner
						William Mathias
				Lift Up Your Heads, *Messiah*		G F Handel
				The Coming		Leon Roberts
	■			Wachet! betet! betet! wachet!, *Cantata 70*		J S Bach
	■			Wachet, betet, seid bereit, *Cantata 70a*		J S Bach
■				Ain'a That Good News		Spiritual, Various
				Additional Music		
■				Above All Praise and All Majesty	OXEA	Felix Mendelssohn
■				Since By Man Came Death	SEW	Thomas Pavlechko
				Cantatas/Major Works		
				116: Du Friedefürst, Herr Jesu Christ		J S Bach

Entrance	Sequence	Offertory	Communion	Postcommunion		H82	WLP	LEVAS II	VF	MHSO	CG descant	Inst descant
		■		■	Alleluia, sing to Jesus (1,3-5) [S]	460,461						
■		■		■	All praise to thee, for thou, O King divine [S]	477					o	
■		■			At the Name of Jesus [S]	435			135		■	
■					Hail to the Lord's Anointed [S]	616						
■			■		Jesus shall reign where'er the sun [S]	544					■	
■				■	King of glory, King of peace [S]	382						
■				■	Lead on, O King eternal [S]	555					o	
				■	Let all mortal flesh keep silence [S]	325						
			■		Soon and very soon			14				
		■			Ye servants of God, your Master proclaim [S]	535						
					Ezekiel 34:11-16,20-24 SC Track/GR Track							
		■			All people that on earth do dwell [P 100]	377,378						■
		■			Before the Lord's eternal throne [P 100]	391						
■	■				Jesus our mighty Lord	478						
■	■				To God with gladness sing [P 95]	399						
					Ephesians 1:15-23							
■		■			All hail the power of Jesus' Name	450,451					■	
					Crown him with many crowns	494					■	
					Hail, thou once despised Jesus	495					■	
		■			He is king of kings, he is Lord of lords			96				
					Lord, enthroned in heavenly splendor	307						
■		■			Rejoice, the Lord is King	481						
					Matthew 25:31-46							
■					Christ is the King, O friends upraise	614						
	■				"Come now, you blessed, eat at my table"					155		
					Cuando el pobre nada tiene / When the poor one who as nothing		802					
■					Father eternal, ruler of creation	573					■	
			■		Lord, whose love through humble service	610						
		■			Praise the Lord through every nation	484,485						
					The King of glory comes					90		
					The servants well-pleasing to God				144			
					Where cross the crowded ways of life	609						

Anthem	Solo	Handbells	Voicing		Collection	Composer
				Collect		
			SA	Create in Me		Paul Bowman
						Johannes Brahms
						Carl F Mueller
				Malachi 3:1-4		
				And He Shall Purify, *Messiah*		G F Handel
			Bass	Thus Saith the Lord, *Messiah*		G F Handel
			Bass	But Who May Abide, *Messiah*		G F Handel
				Psalm 84		
				Behold, O God, Our Defender		Herbert Howells
				How Lovely Are the Temples, *Saul*		G F Handel
				How Lovely Is Thy..., *A German Requiem*		Johannes Brahms
				How Lovely Is Thy Dwelling Place		Multiple
				Jubilate Deo (Ps 100)		Multiple
			SSAATTBB	Lord God of Hosts, How Lovely		Leland Sateren
				O Be Joyful		Multiple
				O How Amiable		John Gardner
			Unison			Maurice Greene
						Thomas Weelkes
			SS			Healey Willan
						Ralph Vaughan Williams
			SSA	Psalm 84		Jan Bender
				Quam dilecta!		Kenneth Leighton
						Charles-Marie Widor
			Contralto	Gott, der Herr, ist Sonn..., *Cantata 79*		J S Bach
				Psalm 24:7-10 (alt)		
				Lift Up Your Heads	16th	John Amner
			SATB/SATB, 3 trp			Jean Berger
						John Blow
						John Carter
						William Croft
			SSAATB			Orlando Gibbons
			SSATBB			Andreas Hammerschmidt
						William Mathias
						Heinrich Schütz
			SSA or SATB			Healey Willan
				Lift Up Your Heads, *Messiah*		G F Handel
			SATB & Unison	The King of Glory		Austin Lovelace
				Hebrews 2:14-18		
				Luke 2:22-40		
				Behold This Child Is Set for the Fall		Heinrich Schütz
				Canticle of Simeon		John Karl Hirten
				Depart in Peace		John Rutter
				Nunc dimittis		Multiple
				Song of Simeon		Alexander Grechaninov
						Jane Marshall
						Alice Parker
						Russell Schulz-Widmar

Entrance	Sequence	Offertory	Communion	Postcommunion		H82	WLP	LEVAS II	VF	MHSO	CG descant	Inst descant
		■			How lovely is thy dwelling-place [P]	517					■	
			■		When candles are lighted on Candlemas Day [S]				31			
					Malachi 3:1-4							
■					Angels from the realms of glory	93						
				■	Love divine, all loves excelling	657						■
					Hebrews 2:14-18							
	■				How bright appears the Morning Star	496,497						
	■				Sing of Mary, pure and lowly	277					■	
	■				The great Creator of the worlds (1-4)	489						
					Luke 2:22-40							
			■		Blessed are the pure in heart	656						
■				■	Christ, whose glory fills the skies	6,7						
					Hail to the Lord who comes	257						
					Let all mortal flesh keep silence	324						■
			■		Lord God, you now have set your servant free	499						
			■		Lord, you have fulfilled your word		891					
		■			Sing we of the blessed Mother	278						
			■		Virgin-born, we bow before thee	258						

Anthem	Solo	Handbells	Voicing		Collection	Composer
				Isaiah 7:10-14		
■				Ecce concipies	CHES	Jacob Handl
■				Ecce virgo concípiet	CHES	Heinrich Isaac
			SSATB			J P Sweelinck
	■			Wie shön leuchtet der..., *Cantata 1*		J S Bach
	■		Alto	Behold, A Virgin Shall Conceive, *Messiah*		G F Handel
	■			What You Goin' to Name the Baby?	SOS	Spiritual, arr Boatner
				Psalm 45		
■				Affrentur regi virgines		Anton Bruckner
■			SSATB	Constitues eos principes		Samuel Wesley
■				My Heart Is Inditing, *Coron. Anthem No 4*		G F Handel
■				O God My King	AFC 1	John Amner
				Psalm 40:5-11		
■				Expectans expectavi		Orlando di Lasso
■						Charles Wood
■				Great and Glorious		F J Haydn
■			2 pt treble	I Waited Patiently for the Lord		Ronald Arnatt
■				Psalm 40		Samuel Adler
■				Thy Law Is within My Heart		Robert Powell
				Canticle 3 or 15 (alt)		
■				Canticle of Mary		Multiple
■				Magnificat		Multiple
■				My Soul Doth Magnify the Lord		Multiple
■				My Soul Magnifies the Lord		Multiple
■				Song of Mary		Multiple
				Hebrews 10:4-10		
■				Salvation Unto Us Has Come	BFAS	J S Bach
				Luke 1:26-38		
■				Ecce virgo concípiet	CHES	Heinrich Isaac
■			SSATB			J P Sweelinck
■				Jesu, dulcis memoria		Multiple
■				Mary Had A Baby		arr William Dawson
■				The Angel Gabriel		Basque Carol, Various
	■		Alto	Behold, A Virgin/O Thou That..., *Messiah*		G F Handel
	■			What You Goin' to Name the Baby?	SOS	Spiritual, arr Boatner

Entrance	Sequence	Offertory	Communion	Postcommunion		H82	WLP	LEVAS II	VF	MHSO	CG descant	Inst descant
	▪				From east to west, from shore to shore (1-3) [S]	77						
		▪			God himself is with us [S]	475					▪	
				▪	Mary, when the angel's voice [S]				64			
	▪				Sing of Mary, pure and lowly [S]	277					▪	
▪					Tell out, my soul, the greatness of the Lord [S]	437,438					▪	
			▪		Virgin-born, we bow before thee [S]	258						
					Isaiah 7:10-14							
	▪				Lo, how a Rose e'er blooming	81						
					Hebrews 10:4-10							
	▪				How bright appears the Morning Star	496,497						
	▪				The great Creator of the worlds (1-4)	489						
					Luke 1:26-38							
	▪				Gabriel's message does away	270						
	▪				Nova, nova	266						
▪					Praise we the Lord this day	267						
			▪		Salamu Maria / Hail Mary, O Mother			51	11			
				▪	Sing we of the blessed Mother	278						
	▪				The angel Gabriel from heaven came	265						
	▪				The Word whom earth and sea and sky	263,264						
	▪				Ye who claim the faith of Jesus	268,269						

Anthem	Solo	Handbells	Voicing			Collection	Composer
				1 Samuel 2:1-10			
■				A New Magnificat			Carolyn Jennings
■				Behold O God Our Defender			John Blow
■				Magnificat			Multiple
			2 pt treble, narr	My Heart Rejoices in the Lord			John Horman
■				My Soul Doth Magnify the Lord			Multiple
■				My Soul Magnifies the Lord			Multiple
				Psalm 113			
				All From the Sun's Uprise		OXEA	Philip Tomblings
				Give Laud Unto the Lord		OXEA	arr Ernest Bullock
				Laudate pueri			Multiple
				Ye Servants of God		OXEA	arr Henry Coleman
				Romans 12:9-16b			
■				Ubi caritas			Maurice Duruflé
				Luke 1:39-57			
■				Canticle of Mary			Multiple
■				Magnificat			Multiple
■				My Soul Doth Magnify the Lord			Multiple
■				My Soul Magnifies the Lord			Multiple
■				Song of Mary			Multiple

Entrance	Sequence	Offertory	Communion	Postcommunion		H82	WLP	LEVAS II	VF	MHSO	CG descant	Inst descant
					Mary, when the angel's voice [S]				64			
■					Sing of Mary, pure and lowly [S]	277					■	
					Sing we of the blessed Mother [S]	278						
			■		Virgin-born, we bow before thee [S]	258						
				■	Ye watchers and ye holy ones	618					■	■
					1 Samuel 2:1-10							
	■				If thou but trust in God to guide thee	635						
	■				Media sida				103			
■					To God with gladness sing	399						
					Romans 12:9-16b							
■					Lord, make us servants of your peace	593						
					Rejoice, ye pure in heart	556,557						■
					Luke 1:39-57							
		■			Jerusalem, my happy home	620					■	
	■	■			My soul gives glory to my God				117			
		■			Tell out, my soul, the greatness of the Lord	437,438					■	
			■		The first one ever, oh, ever to know	673						
	■				Ye who claim the faith of Jesus	268,269						

Anthem	Solo	Handbells	Voicing		Collection	Composer
				Exodus 24:29-35		
■				The Lord Bless You and Keep You		Peter Lutkin
						John Rutter
				Psalm 99		
■			SATB/SATB	Derr Herr ist König		Johann Pachelbel
				Dominus Regnavit		Peter Hallock
■				Let All Mortal Flesh Keep Silence		Edward Bairstow
						Gustav Holst
■				Sanctus		Multiple
■				The Lord is King		David Ashley White
				2 Peter 1:13-21		
■				Christ Is the World's True Light	OXEA	W K Stanton
■				Christ, Whose Glory Fills the Skies	OXCAB	Thomas Armstrong
						T Frederick Candlyn
■				O Paschal Lamp of Radiant Light	AUG	Sam Batt Owens
	Alto			O Thou That Tellest, *Messiah*		G F Handel
■				The Only Son from Heaven	BFAS	J S Bach
				This Is My Beloved Son		Knut Nystedt
				Worthy Is the Lamb, *Messiah*		G F Handel
				Luke 9:28-36		
■				Beautiful Savior		F Melius Christiansen
■				Christ, Whose Glory Fills the Skies	OXCAB	Thomas Armstrong
						T Frederick Candlyn
		■	SAB	Fairest Lord Jesus		Russell Schulz-Widmar
				O nata lux		William Byrd
						William Mathias
						Thomas Tallis
■	Alto			O Thou That Tellest, *Messiah*		G F Handel
				The Spirit of the Lord Is..., *The Apostles*		Edward Elgar
				This Is My Beloved Son		Knut Nystedt
				Of the Father's Heart Begotten	100 CFC, AFC 1	arr David Willcocks
				Additional Music		
■				O Morning Star How Fair and Bright	BFAS	J S Bach
			U & SATB			arr Donald Bursarow
				Te Deum		Multiple
■				The Heavens Are Telling		G F Handel
						F J Haydn
				Cantatas/Major Works		
				130: Herr Gott, dich loben alle wir		J S Bach

Entrance	Sequence	Offertory	Communion	Postcommunion		H82	WLP	LEVAS II	VF	MHSO	CG descant	Inst descant
				■	Let the heav'n light shine on me [S]			174				
					Exodus 34:29-35							
	■				O Zion, tune thy voice	543						
					2 Peter 1:13-21							
				■	Christ is the world's true Light	542						■
■		■			Christ, whose glory fills the skies	6,7						
		■			From God Christ's deity came forth	443						
			■		Jesu, joy of our desiring			75				
■					When morning gilds the skies	427					■	
			■		Yo soy la luz del mundo / I am the world's true light					75		
					Luke 9:28-36							
	■				Christ upon the mountain peak	129,130						
	■				O Light of Light, Love given birth	133,134					■	
		■			O wondrous type, O vision fair	136,137					■	

Anthem	Solo	Handbells	Voicing		Collection	Composer
				Collect		
■				Adoramus te, Christe		Multiple
■				Christus factus est		Multiple
				Isaiah 45:21-25		
■				Above All Praise and All Majesty	OXEA	Felix Mendelssohn
■				At the Name of Jesus		Ralph Vaughan Williams
■				Great and Glorious		F J Haydn
				Psalm 98:1-4, 5-10		
■				Cantate Domino		Multiple
■				Psalm 98		Multiple
■				Sing to the Lord a New Song		Multiple
■				Sing Unto the Lord		Multiple
■				Singet dem Herren		Multiple
				Philippians 2:5-11		
■				Adoramus te, Christe		Multiple
■				At the Name of Jesus		Ralph Vaughan Williams
■				Christus factus est		Multiple
■				Jesu, dulcis memoria		Multiple
■			SAB	Jesus, Name of Wondrous Love		Everett Titcomb
■				Let This Mind Be in You		Lee Hoiby
■				Let Thy Hand..., *Coronation Anthem No 2*		G F Handel
■				Non nobis, Domine		Multiple
■				Praise to You Lord Jesus	CHAN	Heinrich Schütz
				Galatians 6:14-18		
■				Adoramus te, Christe		Multiple
■				Christus factus est		Multiple
■			SSAATTBB	Faithful Cross		Thomas Pavlechko
■				Thee We Adore		T Frederick Candlyn
				John 12:31-36a		
■				As Moses Lifted Up the Serpent		Edward Bairstow
■				Jesus, So Lowly		Harold Friedell
■				Lift Up Your Heads	16th	John Amner
■				Lift Up Your Heads, *Messiah*		G F Handel
■				Sicut Moses serpentem		Heinrich Schütz
■				The Way to Jerusalem		Harold Friedell
■			SATB, vla	Who Is This?		John Ferguson
■			SSATB	Yet a Little While		Knut Nystedt
	■		Bass	The People That Walked in..., *Messiah*		G F Handel

Entrance	Sequence	Offertory	Communion	Postcommunion		H82	WLP	LEVAS II	VF	MHSO	CG descant	Inst descant
				X	Alas! And did my Savior bleed [S]			30				
				X	Beneath the cross of Jesus [S]	498						
		X			Cantad al Señor [P]		786					
				X	Faithful cross, above all other [S]		737					
				X	Jesus, keep me near the cross [S]			29				
		X			New songs of celebration render [P]	413						
			X		On a hill far away stood an old rugged cross [S]			38				
		X			Sing, my tongue the glorious battle [S]	165,166						
		X			The flaming banners of our King [S]	161						
		X			The royal banners forward go [S]	162						
					Isaiah 45:21-25							
		X			Holy God, we praise thy name	366						X
X					How wondrous and great, thy works God of praise!	532,533						
					Philippians 2:5-11							
X					All hail the power of Jesus' Name!	450,451						X
				X	All praise to thee, for thou, O King divine	477					0	
X					At the name of Jesus	435			135		X	X
			X		Cross of Jesus, cross of sorrow	160						
		X			Gracious Spirit, give your servants		782				0	
	X				Jesus! Name of wondrous love!	252						
			X		Morning glory, starlit sky	585					X	
			X		O Spirit of the living God	531						
X					Sing, ye faithful, sing with gladness	492					X	
	X				The head that once was crowned with thorns	483						
			X		What wondrous love is this	439						X
					Galatians 6:14-18							
X					In the cross of Christ I glory	441,442						
		X			Nature with open volume stands	434						
		X			We sing the praise of him who died	471						
	X				When I survey the wondrous cross	474					X	
					John 12:31-36a							
X					Lift high the cross	473						
	X				Lift him up			159				
				X	When Christ was lifted from the earth	603,604					0	

Anthem	Solo	Handbells	Voicing	Title	Collection	Composer
				Revelation 7:9-17		
X				Glory and Worship, *All Night Vigil*		Sergei Rachmaninoff
X				John Saw duh Number		Andre Thomas
X				O quam gloriosum		Multiple
X				These Are They Which Follow the Lamb	AFC 1	John Goss
	X			Wade in the Water		Spiritual, Various
X				Way Over in Beulah Lan'		Stacey Gibbs
						Hall Johnson
X				Worthy Is the Lamb, *Messiah*		G F Handel
				Blessing and Honor		
				Amen		
				Psalm 34:1-10, 22		
X				O Taste and See		Bruce Neswick
X						Ralph Vaughan Williams
X						Eugene Hancock
X				Gustate et videte		Heinrich Isaac
X				Through All the Changing Scenes of Life		Russell Schulz-Widmar
	X			I Will Give Thanks to God Eternally		Heinrich Schütz
				1 John 3:1-3		
X				Behold, What Manner of Love		Carl F Mueller
X						Leo Sowerby
X				See What Love, *St. Paul*		Felix Mendelssohn
	X			Von der Welt verlang' ich nichts, *Cantata 64*		J S Bach
				Matthew 5:1-12		
X				Beatitudes		Russian Chant
X				Blessed Are the Pure in Heart		Walford Davies
X				Blessed Are Those Who Mourn, *Requiem*		Johannes Brahms
X				Blessed Is the Man, *All Night Vigil*		Serge Rachmaninoff
X				Exceeding Glad, *Coronation Anthem No 3*		G F Handel
X				Let Nothing Ever Grieve Thee		Johannes Brahms
X				Soon-Ah Will Be Done		arr William Dawson
X				Swing Low, Sweet Chariot		arr Dale Adelmann
X				The Beatitudes		Micki Grant
				Additional Music		
X				Blessed Are the Dead		Herbert Howells
X				Give Rest O Christ		Russell Schulz-Widmar
X				Holy Is the True Light		Gerald Near
X				In Remembrance		Russell Schulz-Widmar
X				I Heard a Voice from Heaven		John Goss
X				Lo, Round the Throne A Glorious Band	OXCAB	Henry G Ley
X				Man That Is Born of a Woman	OXCAB	Samuel Wesley
X				Now Let Us Praise Famous Men		Ralph Vaughan Williams
X				O God, Whom Saints and Angels...		Bruce Neswick
X				O Heavenly Word, Eternal Light		David Ashley White
X				Peace, Perfect Peace		Libby Larsen
X				Requiem aeternam		Giovanni Francesco Anerio
X			SAB	The Righteous Live for Evermore		Leo Sowerby
X				The Souls of the Righteous		Thomas Pavlechko
X					OXEA	Stanley Marchant
X						Geraint Lewis
X				We Are Not Our Own		Russell Schulz-Widmar
	X			There Is a Spirit in Man	LIFT	Peter Cornelius
				Cantatas/Major Works		
				106: Gottes Zeit ist die allerbeste Zeit		J S Bach
	X		Tenor, Bass	157: Ich lasse dich nicht, du segnest mich...		J S Bach
				198: Trauer Ode: Lass Fürsten...		J S Bach
				Requiem		Multiple

Entrance	Sequence	Offertory	Communion	Postcommunion		H82	WLP	LEVAS II	VF	MHSO	CG descant	Inst descant
				■	All who hunger, gather gladly [P]		761		87	52		
					Christ, the Victorious, give to your servants [S]	358						■
■					For all the saints, who from their labors rest [S]	287					■	
			■		For the bread which you have broken [S]	340,341						
■					For thy dear saints, O Lord [S]	279						
			■		From glory to glory advancing, we praise thee, O Lord [S]	326						
				■	Give rest, O Christ [S]	355						
			■		Give thanks for life [S]		775				o	
					I will bless the Lord at all times [P]		764	154		136		■
			■		Jerusalem, my happy home [S]	620					■	
		■			Let saints on earth in concert sing [S]	526						
			■		No saint on earth lives life to self alone [S]		776					
					Revelation 7:9-17							
			■		All glory be to God on high	421						
■	■				By all your saints still striving (All Saints' Day)	231,232					■	■
					Give us the wings of faith to rise	253						
■					Glorious things of thee are spoken	522,523					■	
		■			Hark! The sound of holy voices	275						
■					Hearken to the anthem glorious	240,241						
■					Holy God, we praise thy Name	366						■
			■		Jerusalem the golden	624						
			■		My God, how wonderful thou art	642						
		■			Nature with open volume stands	434						
■					O God, we praise thee and confess	364						
■					Sing alleluia forth in duteous praise	619	777					
					We shall overcome			227				
					We sing of the saints (All Saints)					118		
					We'll understand it better by and by			207				
■					Who are these like stars appearing	286					■	
			■		Ye holy angels bright	625						
■					Ye servants of God, your Master proclaim	535						
■					Ye watchers and ye holy ones	618					■	
					1 John 3:1-3							
■					Ancient of Days, who sittest throned in glory	363						
					Children of the heavenly Father			213				
					Jesus, the very thought of thee	642						
					We are all children of the Lord					105		
					Matthew 5:1-12							
	■				Beati		828					
					Blessed are the poor in spirit					74		
■					Blessed Jesus, at thy word	440						
					Blest are the pure in heart	656						
		■			Gracious Spirit, give your servants		782				o	
					Lord, make us servants of your peace	593						
		■			Rejoice, ye pure in heart	556,557						■
					Remember your servants, Lord	560						
			■		Tis the gift to be simple	554						
					You shall cross the barren desert		811					
					At Baptism:							
					All who believe and are baptized	298						
					Baptized in water	294	767	121				
					Come away to the skies	213						
					I believe in God Almighty		768,769					
					You have put on Christ					122		
					You're called by name, forever loved		766					

o Same tune, but not text [S] Seasonal [C] Collect [P] Psalm [GR] Gospel-related [SC] Semi-continuous

Anthem	Solo	Handbells	Voicing		Collection	Composer
				Deuteronomy 8:7-18		
				Benedic anima mea	CHES	Claudin de Sermisy
				Bless the Lord, O My Soul	OXEA	C Armstrong Gibbs
						Ippolitov-Ivanov
						Austin Lovelace
			Unison	Blessed be my Lord		Doug Wagner
				Not Only Unto Him/Bless Now…, *St. Paul*		Felix Mendelssohn
			SATB/SATB	O Bless the Lord		Giovanni Gabrieli
				O Comfort Now My People	SEW	Thomas Pavlechko
				O Lord, I Will Praise Thee	OXEA	Gordon Jacob
			Unison	O Praise the Lord		Maurice Greene
				Praise the Lord, O My Soul		Thomas Tomkins
				Psalm 65		
			Unison, inst	God's Joyful Harvest		Robert J Powell
				Jubilate Deo		Multiple
				O Be Joyful		Multiple
				Praise Is Due to You, O God in Zion		William Mathias
				Praise Is Your Right, O God, in Zion		Claude Goudimel, ed Proulx
				Thou, Oh God, Art Praised in Sion		Malcolm Boyle
						David Willcocks
			SSA or SATB	Thou Visitest the Earth	OXCAB	Maurice Greene
			2 pt treble			Alec Rowley
				To You Our Praise Is Due in Zion, O God		Colin Mawby
				2 Corinthians 9:6-15		
				O Taste and See		Bruce Neswick
						Ralph Vaughan Williams
				Oculi omnium		Charles Wood
				The Eyes of All Wait Upon Thee		Jean Berger
						William Harris
						Gerald Near
			Unison			Richard Proulx
				Luke 17:11-19		
				Now Thank We All Our God	BFAS	J S Bach
						Healey Willan
				Nun danket alle Gott SATB/SATB		Johann Pachelbel
				O Lord, Increase My Faith		Henry Loosemoore
				Thank You Lord for One More Day		Andrae Crouch
						Kirk Franklin/Mary Mary
				Additional Music		
			SAB	All From the Sun's Uprise	OXEA	Philip Tomblins
				All People That on Earth Do Dwell	AFC 1	Thomas Tallis
	▨		SAB	Autumn Carol		Russell Schulz-Widmar
				E'en So Lord Jesus Quickly Come		Paul Manz
				Laud Ye the Name of the…, *All Night Vigil*		Sergei Rachmaninoff
				The Old Hundredth Psalm Tune		Ralph Vaughan Williams
				Every Day Will I Give Thanks	LIFT	G F Handel
				Trust in the Lord, *Light of the World*	LIFT	Arthur Sullivan
				Cantatas/Major Works		
				29: Wir danken dir, Gott, wir danken dir		J S Bach
				192: Nun danket alle Gott		J S Bach

	Entrance	Sequence	Offertory	Communion	Postcommunion		H82	WLP	LEVAS II	VF	MHSO	CG descant	Inst descant
						All people that on earth do dwell [S]	377,378						
						As those of all those first fruits brought [S]	705						
						Come, ye thankful people, come [S]	290						
						For the beauty of the earth [S]	416						
						For the fruit of all creation [S]	424						
						Give thanks to the Lord for he is good [S]			93				
						Glory, love, and praise, and honor [S]	300						
						Grateful praise and hymns of adoration [S]				114			
						Let all things now living [S]				107			
						Now thank we all our God [S]	396,397						
						Praise to God, immortal praise [S]	288						
						We gather together to ask the Lord's blessing [S]	433						
						We plow the fields and scatter	291						
						We thank God for giving us life [S]					137		
						When all thy mercies, O my God [S]	415						
						Deuteronomy 8:7-18							
						God, my King, thy might confessing	414						
						O give thanks to the Lord					138		
						O God of Bethel, by whose hand	709						
						2 Corinthians 9:6-15							
						Father, we thank thee who hast planted	302,303						
						Not here for high and holy things	9						
						Thank you for the gift of Jesus					139		
						We plow the fields and scatter	291						
						What gift can we bring, what present, what token?				118			
						Luke 17:11-19							
						Thine arm, O Lord, in days of old	567						
						When all thy mercies, O my God	415						